NOWHERE

WITH

YOU

The East Coast Anthems of
Joel Plaskett,
The Emergency
and Thrush Hermit

JOSH O'KANE

For two doting Dorothys
from Chatham, N.B.

There's a rainbow in Toronto
Where the Maritimers are bold
They always get a pot full
But they never get a pot of gold

— Stompin' Tom Connors, "To It and at It," 1973

All my friends, where did they go?
To Montreal, Toronto

— Joel Plaskett, "Work Out Fine," 2003

CONTENTS

AN INTRODUCTION

THE GUYS FROM Sloan were back for the holidays, and word had it they'd be at Dave Marsh's new house for a party. Even though the Halifax drummer's place had no furniture, Joel Plaskett had every reason to be there: it was close to home, his mentors in Sloan had long ago moved to Toronto, and in recent months Marsh had become a close confidant and musical partner. But instead, Plaskett got into his green '69 Pontiac Parisienne and spent the last few hours of the 20th century driving to Cape Breton.

The overhyped end of the millennium coincided, for Plaskett, with a more literal end. His band, Thrush Hermit, had played their final show and broken up just three weeks earlier. Playing in that band was the only job the 24-year-old had ever had; he'd been singing and playing guitar in it for a decade, alongside his best friends Rob Benvie and Ian McGettigan. The band had spent the '90s morphing from prank-calling kids to scrappy Superchunk disciples to hard-rock revivalists, drawing heaps of music-industry attention along the way.

This hinted at a long career trajectory for the Thrush Hermit crew, whose network of connections read like a checklist of '90s cool: they were discovered by a guy who helped give the Wu-Tang Clan their first publishing deal; recorded with the minds behind classic Pavement, Nirvana, and Beck albums; and retained the Beastie Boys' lawyer. But a checklist doesn't entertain context, and in reality, they had a tough time making it in entertainment. Thrush Hermit's story turned out to be one of almosts — of a band defeated by bad timing, a shifting major-label ecosystem, and themselves, thanks to an indie-or-bust ethos and democratic design.

Before the final show, discussing the band's breakup with the *Toronto Star*, Plaskett was worried about his post-Hermit career. "I want to find a way to make it in Canada. But how do you continue to do cool things within a small scene?" he asked. "In Canada, I don't know if you can." Playing music, though, was all he knew. And he was stubborn. By New Year's Eve, he was done questioning himself. He didn't want to take time off before starting another band, and he had zero intention of leaving Halifax or Nova Scotia behind, either. The place had given him everything, even if staying there, far from any major music centre, had its setbacks. If he was going to keep making music, it was going to be on his own terms — how he wanted to, what he wanted to, and where he wanted to. Musicians around Halifax had already figured this out about Plaskett, and there was much talk behind his back about who would get to be a part of his next project. But by New Year's Eve, Plaskett already knew exactly who he wanted to play with. He'd nailed down a drummer: Dave Marsh, the scene veteran who was partying with members of Sloan that night. Marsh had drummed in the five-piece band Plaskett put together to play shows supporting *In Need of Medical Attention*, the country-flavoured solo record he'd just put out after his girlfriend got him hooked on Lefty Frizzell. The pair quickly formed a musical bond, and, when Thrush Hermit was in its death throes, Plaskett turned to Marsh to keep his rock 'n' roll dream alive. Marsh, in turn, mentioned that Tim Brennan, a former bandmate and a friend since his '80s punk days, might make a fine bassist for a three-piece band.

Brennan had moved away long before, living in New York and Toronto to study photography. Plaskett had actually already met him — he'd done photography for Thrush Hermit's 1995 EP *The Great Pacific Ocean* — but they'd never played music together. He was, in Plaskett's words, "super cool," a no-nonsense bassist who could channel Paul Simonon at one moment and Waylon Jennings the next. Like the guys in Sloan, Brennan happened to be back in Nova Scotia for the holidays — and rumour had it he'd be moving to Halifax in the new year. So Plaskett spent New Year's Eve in his car driving to Inverness, Brennan's Cape Breton hometown.

As cruel as east-coast winters can be, the weather was clear that day, though the roads were a little dusty as they headed for the winding hills of Cape Breton Island. Plaskett is a tall man — about six-foot-three, though he tends to hunch over — but the boat-sized Parisienne had more than enough room for him and his carmates. Sitting

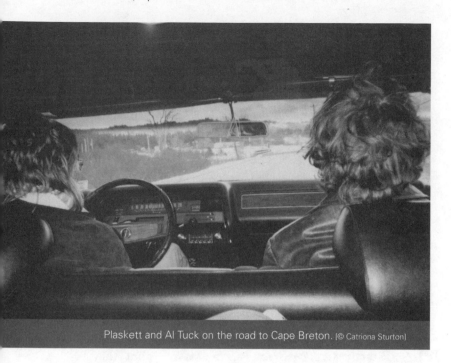

Plaskett and Al Tuck on the road to Cape Breton. [© Catriona Sturton]

shotgun was Al Tuck, a respected and well-connected craftsman among Halifax songwriters, whom Plaskett looked up to. They mirrored each other on the drive: two brown coats with matching brown shags on either side of the Pontiac's green leather bench seat. It might as well have been the '70s. On the long drives there and back, they listened to Led Zeppelin and the Rolling Stones, arguing over their respective prowesses; the older, gravel-voiced Tuck argued for the Stones, while Plaskett, in spite of his indelible, childlike grin, fought zealously for Team Zep. In the backseat, Plumtree bassist Catriona Sturton, Tuck's then-girlfriend, struggled to get a word in edgewise. She had slightly better luck eventually, turning the conversation to traditional folk and musical ambitions. Ambition, after all, was the reason they were on the road in the first place.

They checked in at the Jingles Motel and headed to the Brennan family homestead. New Year's was mostly a family affair, but it was a classic east-coast kitchen party; Plaskett and his entourage were welcomed warmly. Everyone took turns at the household piano. There was, according to one account, a bottle of Jameson going around. The oft-whispered conspiracy theory that a computer glitch might shut down the world at midnight did not particularly weigh on the party, though an unknown guest surreptitiously filled the bathtub with water, just in case. Kids ran through the house, but by the time everyone gathered around the basement TV to watch the midnight fireworks in Halifax, they were all but asleep. At some point, Plaskett and Brennan began to talk shop — and yes, it turned out, Brennan *was* moving back to Halifax.

Plaskett made his offer. "When you come back, man, wanna play bass?"

Nova Scotia is a small place, and Halifax is even smaller. Plaskett's reputation preceded him; Brennan knew the kid was born to perform. Being in his band would be one hell of a party — especially with Marsh, one of his best friends, behind the kit. The decision was easy.

"Sure. Absolutely."

And so it was, without hesitation, that Plaskett had himself a new bassist, a new band, and a new motivation to make music right at home. Less than a month after Thrush Hermit clipped their own wings, the Joel Plaskett Emergency power trio was born.

WITH THE SAFETY blanket of his last band cast away, Plaskett had to start fresh, recording with friends on a shoestring budget, promoting shows alone, and handling his own business affairs. He'd drive for whole days to play to handfuls of people, stay up for nights on end to perfect his recordings, and take a square job to pay for all of it. But his tale is one of incessant hustle and slow, but eventual, payoff. First came management, a label, and Juno nominations; then a solo album, a rock opera, and a triple record, each expanding his live repertoire in distinct ways and finally nabbing him a Juno; then his own label and recording studio, letting him make all the music he wants, for both himself and his friends. Along the way, he's become a touring machine. He's played rooms across Canada, from empty bars in Fredericton to a packed Massey Hall in Toronto, while fans and the media toss around nicknames for him like folk hero, indie darling, and national treasure.

That he's pulled this off while staying at home in Nova Scotia is a feat in and of itself. His reason for doing so is simple — "I never really wanted to be anywhere else" — but the odds were stacked against him from the start. By the time they'd broken up, Thrush Hermit was one of the last bands standing after a wave of music-industry attention swept Canada's east coast in the '90s. That wave was a first for a region that has historically been on the country's cultural, geographical, and political periphery — as Sloan best put it, it's twice removed from everything else happening in the world. Save for a handful of Celtic- and traditional-influenced musicians, most local artists who'd ever sought success had moved away. The '90s east-coast "pop explosion" lured in labels like Geffen and eager post-Nirvana Sub Pop — but if there really was an explosion, it was that of a bubble bursting too soon. The bands that spearheaded the hype either split or split town: the Hardship Post, the Super Friendz, Jale, and Eric's Trip broke up, while the members of Sloan gradually snuck off to Toronto. Though Thrush Hermit had a longer run than many of their peers, they spent most of their heyday, from 1993 to 1999, struggling to get off the ground.

This obviously set a difficult precedent for home-town success. But while things didn't work out for Thrush Hermit, they remain a cult favourite for thousands of fans, and Plaskett's time in the band helped him build both a strong network of supporters and a critically acclaimed songwriting prowess. He's since used both to great advantage, fronting the Emergency — and establishing a parallel career as a respected solo singer-songwriter — for more than twice as long as he played full-time in Thrush Hermit. It took more than a decade to build his career, but by the time he released 2015's *The Park Avenue Sobriety Test*, he'd taken home a Juno, a CBC Radio 3 Lifetime Achievement Award, a Gold record, and more than 20 East Coast Music Awards, all while putting thousands of shows under his belt and nearly half a million kilometres on his old '95 Chevy Suburban.

Plaskett's road-warrior mentality has helped him capture the hearts of all kinds of Canadians, playing every nook and cranny from coast to coast to coast, winning over each fan one at a time. And he's done it while writing about what he knows best: the east coast. Plaskett's kitsch-free

Canadiana proves that you can make acclaimed pop and rock music about Atlantic Canada without actually having to leaving the place. At concerts in cities like Calgary, east-coast expats literally thank him for staying home. At Toronto shows, when he asks if there are any Maritimers in the crowd, the room erupts in screams. He has convinced fans across the country — including people who've never set foot in Canada's four easternmost provinces — to romanticize life among the island girls and the harbour boys, and to help him, tongue-in-cheek, mock friends for shipping off to Montreal and Toronto, even if that's where he's playing. It's little surprise, then, that the province of Nova Scotia actually licenses his music for tourism ads. Plaskett's music has become a crucial, accessible, award-winning document of — and argument against — the generations-long exodus from Atlantic Canada.

This, he argues, is unintentional; he simply writes what he knows. But in doing so, he's become Nova Scotia's smaller-scale, if much lankier, Bruce Springsteen — a songwriter with a great live reputation whose characters romanticize a place that many chide and many more leave behind. Call it Nova Jersey. Like Springsteen, Plaskett has a sonic duality, coupling a sensitive solo side with a shredding rock repertoire, and puts on a beloved live show no matter which sound he's leaning toward on a given night. Perhaps the most important parallel with the Boss, though, is in Plaskett's work ethic: he's spent more than two decades relentlessly making music in the studio and on the road, with many more decades to go. From his oft-ignored corner of the world, he's drawn his own roadmap for success.

REWIND, REWIND, REWIND

COINCIDENCES CAN BE pretty great. On a sunny September Saturday just after moving to Toronto, I stayed in bed until 3 p.m., because I had nothing to do. I had come here for a job and, for the first time I could remember, had no work to deal with on the weekend. But I also had no one to hang out with, because I'd left most of my friends behind in New Brunswick a month earlier. Since I'd just bought a turntable, I finally convinced myself to get out of bed to go find a vinyl copy of Joel Plaskett Emergency's *Ashtray Rock*. I'd spent much of my younger life believing a foolish theory that Maritimers only liked music made in the Maritimes to justify their own cultural relevance, not because the music was actually good. *Ashtray Rock* was the chief album that changed my mind. It wasn't just a great rock record that I needed to add to my collection; after leaving the east coast, it had taken on a whole new life for me. It began to feel like a document of growing up on Canada's east coast — of

its brutal winters, of its summer nights spent running off
to party in the woods, of its constant outflux of people. I'd
listen to the mp3 version front to back as I took the bus,
then the subway, to work. "The Instrumental" would begin
as I got off, six stops east; I'd emerge onto Yonge Street as
the lap steel kicked in and the record's duelling protagonists
got a postcard from the girl who got away — who moved
away. I'd get to the office listening to "Soundtrack for the
Night," an ode to not knowing what you've got until it's
gone. Its story was fiction, but after the move, *Ashtray Rock*
was among the most relatable records I'd ever heard.

So I hauled myself out of the tiny room in the apartment
I rented with strangers and began my search. No shops on
Bloor Street had *Ashtray Rock*, so I took a streetcar south to
Queen West. First store, nothing. Second store, nothing. I
gave up, picked up some other records, and grabbed another
streetcar home.

It was standing room only. I wound up near the rear exit.
As we pulled up to the next stop, a tall, familiar-looking guy
hopped on.

It was Joel Plaskett.

Was it? Actually? *Nah. Wait — maybe?* We hit the next
stop, a dozen people shuffled off, and the man walked far-
ther back. *It's definitely him.* Soon enough, we were standing
next to each other.

I froze. *Should I just stand here?* This guy's music was the
reason I got out of bed that day. *Ugh.* The coincidence was
too much to handle.

Well, fuck it. "Excuse me — are you Joel Plaskett?"

"Yeah, man. What's your name?"

Of course he was this friendly. I told him my name and, unable to handle silence, started throwing him questions. Was he in town for the Polaris Music Prize gala on Monday? Yeah, actually — he'd been invited to play songs from his *Ashtray Rock* follow-up, 2009's *Three*, which was shortlisted that year. Played anywhere cool lately? Definitely — he'd just come from a quick gig in New York, and before that he was actually in Fredericton, the city I'd left the previous month; my friends had seen him play a few days earlier. After a little more small talk, I held up my bag of records and confessed that I'd been looking for *Ashtray Rock*.

"Oh, sorry, man. We sold out of those on the first tour. But I might press it again someday."

My face probably lit up. And then I realized I'd missed my stop four blocks ago. I wished him good luck at the Polaris Prize, got off the streetcar, and texted about 4,000 people.

Three didn't win the Polaris, but that streetcar encounter made me circle back to it anyway, and I came to love it as much as I did *Ashtray Rock*. At first, it mostly served me as a breakup album, for both a girl and a place; the record is, after all, about leaving someone and somewhere behind. But with enough listens — and, for a while, a mended relationship — the record's whole picture became clearer. It's about coming home, too, and embracing what you've got and where you're from. Soon I was seeing bigger pictures across Plaskett's whole catalogue — crystal-clear portraits of life on the east coast, of growing up there, of leaving there, of coming home. The ghost of geography infects his oeuvre, from its friendly barroom tales and harbour-town stories

Plaskett in the mid-2000s. [© Ingram Barss]

to too-familiar ruminations over one's place in the world. The frustrations of leaving and loss, I soon recognized, were sprinkled throughout his entire body of work. The themes popped up constantly: in Thrush Hermit songs like "I'm Sorry If Your Heart Has No More Room" and the breakup bookend "Before You Leave"; in the loved-ones-long-gone songs of the Emergency's *Truthfully, Truthfully*; and in the metaphoric road trips of *La De Da* and *Three*.

As I explored Plaskett's catalogue with fresh ears, the prospect of living in Toronto for the long-term was becoming more of a reality, even though I was identifying as a New Brunswicker, and a Maritimer, far more than ever before. His lyrics started to carry more bite, like in "Work Out Fine," where he calls out friends for shipping off to Montreal and Toronto, and in "Love This Town," where he jokes about just how easy — and fun — it can be to hold a grudge against them. Like thousands before me, I'm living out a theme that's been an undercurrent for much of Plaskett's work: living well, for many, means leaving home. And like any good lapsed Catholic, my internalized guilt occasionally rises up, reminding me that I've left the place with which I most strongly identify. I fly the flag, but it doesn't match my mailing address. Over time, this cognitive dissonance just keeps getting wider. I'm prouder than I ever have been of where I'm from, but my roots elsewhere keep getting deeper. My love for home is complicated, but as somebody once pointed out, free and easy's overrated.

LIKE MUCH OF Canadian art, there's an inextricable connection between Plaskett's work and its sense of place. He's a great proponent of regionalism, of fostering the history and stories that make a place what it is. Atlantic Canada's sense of place in the world is inexorably shaped by distance. The closest Canadian metropolis, Montreal, is at least a 10-hour drive for most East Coasters, and the rest of the vast, culturally unique province of Quebec sits in between. This instills a fierce sense of independence in Atlantic Canada, even though that same distance breeds an economic dependence on the rest of the country. East Coasters will tell you that there is no place in the world as great as our home, and in many ways, we are correct. It is a place steeped in history and surrounded by nature, the people are among the friendliest in the world, and the cost of living remains bafflingly low.

But boosterism rarely acknowledges broader contexts. As Canada's major hubs developed along the St. Lawrence River and its watershed centuries ago, the Atlantic region was established, largely, as a place to pass through or pass by, onto the rest of the country. The prospect of leaving home, then, is something East Coasters have long had to grapple with. The prolific author and journalist Harry Bruce — who bucked migration trends by moving from his birthplace, Toronto, to his ancestral home of Nova Scotia — wrote in his east-coast epistle *Down Home*: "Maritimers, more than other Canadians, have had to keep their eyes on the horizons, and Leaving Home has long outlasted the golden age of sail as part of their heritage. It is as Down-Home as a clambake at dusk, complete with Moosehead ale." And Gary Burrill, who edited the now-defunct *New Maritimes* magazine, met so many Maritimers who had moved away to Ontario, Alberta, and "the Boston States" that he compiled a whole book about their stories, arguing that leaving is an "inseparable" part of the regional identity. In one sense, this isn't all bad: tension fuels art, and on the east coast, the theme of going away has inspired songwriters for at least 130 years. While previous generations of musicians wrote straightforward songs about nostalgia and shuttered industry, today's pop recognizes this reality with a tongue-in-cheek flair, from Plaskett's less-than-subtle expat chiding in "Work Out Fine" to the name of electronic producer Ryan Hemsworth's early album *Can Anything Good Come From Halifax?* Beneath the jabs, though, the harsh reality remains: today, Canada's most eastern provinces have the smallest populations in the country, while New Brunswick, Nova Scotia, and Prince Edward Island have the lowest gross domestic product per capita — which is a nice way of saying they have a measurably low standard of living. People have flocked from low-density communities to big cities for centuries, but in Atlantic Canada, the numbers give them an extra push.

This context gives greater meaning to Plaskett's success as an artist living on the east coast. It's also why his concerts sell so well in cities like Toronto and Calgary, where east-coast diaspora head in droves. "Atlantic Canadians want to support artists from home," his manager Sheri Jones once said, "because they will take any opportunity to be reminded of home." Ontario and Alberta are the ostensibly greener pastures where youth, talent, and labour tend to seek work and like-minded people. Often, those like-minded people are other Maritimers, meeting through well-timed introductions and happy accidents. Harry Bruce once described Maritimers as "like a motorcycle gang," banding together in spite of our inherent stubbornness and infighting; never do we band together more tightly than when away from home. And luckily for us, we have Plaskett's music. He isn't the relative at Christmas dinner nagging us to move back east. He's a nationally beloved artist that transcended the barrier of geography to tell stories from a corner of the world that sheds more storytellers every day.

The culture of leaving that set this stage stretches back for centuries. The region has a history of displacing its own, actually, that goes further back in time than the idea of Canada itself. Since about 1500 c.e., people there have shouldered the consequences of directives issued from plush rooms in distant capitals in the names of colonialism, bottom lines, and Canadian unity. No wonder the kids don't want to live there.

As soon as explorers like Cabot and Cartier stumbled across the region that would become Atlantic Canada, the wheels were set in motion. First, the native Mi'kmaq, Wolastoqiyik, Passamaquoddy, Beothuk, and other First Nations peoples were slowly, methodically exploited, displaced, and killed as Europeans began to arrive. The early French Acadian settlers were next. In the 1750s, nearly 11,000 of them were deported as far as Louisiana and the Falkland Islands after new British rulers demanded allegiance or exile in what's been called *le Grand Dérangement*.

After generations of French and English power struggles, things settled by the mid-19th century; the region flourished with industry, thanks in large part to shipping and shipbuilding, and the population reached 800,000 by 1861.* But the east-coast colonies — eventually provinces — were slow to adapt to industrial changes, and people soon began to trickle away. As the world's ships moved to steel

---

* The boom was only for settlers, of course — the Aboriginal population in the Maritimes had by then shrunk to 3,000, mostly on reserves.

and steam, the Atlantic provinces stuck with wood and wind, and their ports were eclipsed by more forward-thinking ones. The lack of strong rail infrastructure, too, helped choke out the region's shipping hubs as cargo-bound vessels instead went to the U.S. or down the St. Lawrence River. By the time Confederation was enacted — originating, partly, as a band-aid effort by the Atlantic colonies to secure funding to strengthen its rail networks — the region had lost its chance to be an economic entry point to Canada. Instead, power, people, and industrial centres further concentrated along the St. Lawrence and its tentacled corridors. Maritimers started leaving home by the thousands. One historian called it an "exodus" that took on "the characteristics of a mass migration." Another called it a "decapitation" of Maritime society. From 1851 to 1931, more than 600,000 people left the Maritimes; while there was some immigration, it was a net loss of 460,000 people. Tragedies over those decades only exacerbated the problem. The Great Fire of Saint John in 1877 burned two-fifths of the New Brunswick city to the ground, grinding to a halt any chance of the city becoming a competitive shipping hub. And in Halifax, roughly 2,000 people died and the city's north end was levelled in 1917, when a French munitions ship blew up in the city's harbour during the First World War.

By the turn of the century, the pressure to move away had become ingrained in the public consciousness, and original English songs began to emerge about leaving home. One, "Prince Edward Isle, Adieu," is a flippant takedown of Confederation that sees several characters leave the island behind: "'Tis clear, they can't stay here / For work to do there's none." Sometime around the turn of the century, a similar song emerged from Nova Scotia. Folklorist Helen Creighton came across several versions of "Farewell to Nova Scotia" while researching along the province's eastern shore: "Farewell to Nova Scotia, the sea-bound coast / May your mountains dark and dreary be / For when I am far away on the briny ocean tossed / Will you ever heave a sigh or a wish for me?" It's become a popular traditional song, covered by artists like Gordon Lightfoot and the Real McKenzies.

By the time Newfoundland joined Canada in 1949, the Atlantic provinces were firmly established as the kid brother at the end of the table: scrawny, begging for the country's leftovers, and aggravating to the adults who were trying to make serious conversation. Nearly 100,000 people left the region each decade from the 1940s to the 1960s, for familiar reasons, writes public policy researcher Donald Savoie: "continuing to go down the road to Central Canada to secure a job." And while immigrants landed in Atlantic Canada, many of them were just stopping by on their way somewhere else.

Canada brought in equalization payments to have-not provinces in the 1950s, but they focused more on public services than the economy, and not much changed on the east coast. Some academics literally started to use the term "Maritimization" to describe the threat of broader economic marginalization. Acknowledging relative federal inaction toward the region's generally lower quality of life, economic historian David Alexander once suggested that Atlantic Canadians might have to seek a "new notion of happiness" and look within the region, not abroad, to measure their standard of living — and that the happiness they'd find might not be all that happy. The struggle has continued into the 21st century. The region grew less than one-tenth of a percent between 2011 and 2015, compared to the national rate of 4.4 percent. Meanwhile, 10 percent of the local labour force is unemployed, versus Canada's average of 6.9 percent. In other words, it's still tough for the region to keep people and keep them working.

IN THE 20TH century, all of this began to seep into popular culture. Donald Shebib's critically acclaimed 1970 film *Goin' Down the Road* told the story of two down-on-their-luck Cape Breton boys moving to Toronto for work after years of "driving up and down Main Street looking for something you know damn well ain't there." It's a beloved film — and one of Joel Plaskett's favourites — but it's among the grimmest pop portraits of the region's never-ending exodus. Shebib's Cape Breton is all dilapidated houses and broken-down boats, and in Toronto, things get worse for the boys — they can barely find work and resort to theft to stay alive. After the credits roll, a disclaimer appears: "The characters in this photoplay are fictional and any similarity to actual persons living or dead is purely coincidental." But there are thousands, if not hundreds of thousands, of people for whom this story isn't fiction.

As broadcast and recording technology began to democratize music in the mid-20th century, Atlantic Canadian musicians had the chance to become more ambitious. For those like fiddling folk icon Don Messer, that meant building a career at home and broadcasting shows across Canada, which he did for decades on on CBC Radio and Television. For others, life went full circle. Saint John's Ken Tobias, who wrote a Top-10 Billboard hit and recorded with Righteous Brother Bill Medley, moved to cities like Montreal and Los Angeles only to come back to a quieter career in New Brunswick after a life of touring on next to no money. But most Maritime musicians who made a dent in music history settled far from home. Early country star Wilf Carter, born and raised in Nova Scotia, was banished from home after deciding to master the genre's new yodelling craze as a teen, much to the chagrin of his staunchly religious Baptist minister father. He eventually found his way to Alberta wheat fields, Montreal recording studios, and New York radio stations. In the Big Apple, a secretary bestowed him a new name: Montana Slim. He went on to spend much of his life in Alberta and the U.S. Hank Snow, 10 years Carter's junior and a Jimmie Rodgers fanatic, chased happiness from Brooklyn, Nova Scotia, all the way to Nashville, Tennessee, on the invitation of Ernest Tubb. There, he became a regular at the Grand Ole Opry, thanks to the success of songs like 1950's "I'm Movin' On," which became a country standard and was eventually covered by the likes of Ray Charles and the Rolling Stones. That song might imply leaving home behind, but Snow would later rhapsodize the province he left more directly in 1968's "My Nova Scotia Home," waxing romantic about Cape Breton sunrises and the blue Atlantic sky.

In May 1972, *Maclean's* magazine published two side-by-side profiles of Maritime artists who'd shipped away.

One featured Snow, framed around his choice to live in Tennessee; the sub-headline read "Why Nova Scotia's Hank Snow Ain't Comin' Home No More." Snow wrapped his personal story around escaping the isolation of Canada's east coast: he may have missed his Nova Scotia home, but leaving it, he said, was necessary. "I figgered it would just be so wonderful not to have to jump on an old train and ride 1,000 miles from Halifax to Montreal settin' up, just to make a record."

The issue's cover star was Anne Murray, who had become the first Maritimer to climb the pop charts with her recording of Gene MacLellan's "Snowbird," a song about leaving home after heartbreak. The story, "What Upper Canada Has Done to Anne Murray," opens with a ride on the rails from Halifax to Toronto: "The train is not unlike the country it runs through. . . . It's full of beautiful reasons for leaving." In her early career, Murray stocked her management with East Coasters, and they became affectionately known as the Maritime Mafia. Toronto, to them, was a compromise: they may have missed home, but it was where work had taken them. Murray had success before leaving the east coast — "Snowbird" was a million-selling single before she headed west — but she needed to live closer to the music industry if she wanted to keep any forward momentum. Without a strong follow-up to "Snowbird," she worried of having to return to "the relative Maritime obscurity from whence I'd come."

Upper Canada became a necessary pilgrimage for rock, country, and folk musicians, too. The young men of April Wine left the Halifax area for Montreal in early 1970, just five months after forming. "We almost had to move away," says founding bassist Jim Henman, who left the band in its early days to return to Nova Scotia. "It was our goal. I can't remember anybody from that period who actually accomplished any type of success by staying here as their home base." Some songwriters put the Maritimes front and centre in their music long after they'd left it behind. Stompin' Tom Connors was born in Saint John, New Brunswick, and raised in Skinners Pond, Prince Edward Island, and while he mostly lived on the road and in Ontario, he'd always introduce himself as "Stompin' Tom from Skinners Pond." Connors would fill Toronto's Horseshoe Tavern with Maritimers in the late '60s and early '70s, playing songs like the cutesy P.E.I. potato anthem "Bud the Spud." But he was not all playfulness. "New Brunswick and Mary," for instance, addresses the heartbreak of a man bound for the Prairies, while "To It and at It" explores the stories of people from all corners of the Maritimes trying — and failing — to find a better life in Toronto. The song even became a recurring punch line in SCTV's 1982 parody of Shebib's *Goin' Down the Road*, in which John Candy and Joe Flaherty play a lawyer and surgeon from Moncton who, despite their lucrative jobs, still go to Toronto for work. And that skit, in turn, helped inspire a YouTube series called *Just Passing Through*, in which two Prince Edward Islanders get stuck in Toronto and struggle to adapt to its culture, all while on their way to find work in the most recent Maritime expat Mecca: Alberta.

Ron Hynes lived and died in Newfoundland, but his most famous song, "Sonny's Dream," came to him while he was far away in Western Canada, travelling by bus in 1976. The song became a folk standard, but it's a familiar east-coast tale: a farming mother worries that she'll lose her son to the adventures of the sea and the world beyond it. The east coast even inspired songwriters who'd been born elsewhere. Stan Rogers lived most of his life in southern Ontario, but he built a reputation in folk circles as "Maritime Stan," thanks to his Atlantic-focused debut, *Fogarty's Cove*. He romanticized his family's roots on Nova Scotia's eastern shore and openly resented the fact he wasn't born there. Separation and loss are constant themes in Rogers's music, especially in the Maritime context, with songs like "The Idiot," about a man working in Alberta and longing for home after making the expedition west. Alongside Cape Bretoner John Allan Cameron, Rogers is regularly credited with popularizing the Celtic-influenced east-coast traditional folk sound. More importantly, Rogers's success helped demonstrate that original music could be written within the framework of this genre and thrive.

Soon after Rogers's death in 1983, record labels began pillaging the region for all the Celtic-flavoured and traditional-influenced acts they could get their hands on, sending the likes of the Rankin Family, Great Big Sea, the Barra MacNeils, Rita MacNeil, Natalie MacMaster, and Ashley MacIsaac up the Canadian charts. To the rest of the world, theirs are the sounds most closely associated with Atlantic Canada. But that hardly paints a whole picture of the region's culture — especially so in the past quarter-century. Traditional music basks in history rather than embracing the present. It's safe. With the exception of daring experimenters like MacIsaac, the genre revels in conformity, rarely pushing boundaries or exploring new sounds, even when crossing over into pop. By the late '70s, artists that were doing something far more forward-looking began to emerge on the east coast. The pressure to leave Atlantic Canada still hung in the air, and it still sometimes came across in lyrics, but the music sounded different than ever before. As is often the case, punk can take credit for shifting the creative zeitgeist.

THE REGION'S FIRST punk scenes sprouted up in isolation from one another, but were each crucial stepping stones toward sustainable independent music communities. Moncton's Mark Gaudet, later a force in the bands Eric's Trip and Elevator, started the city's first punk band — named, aptly, Punks — in 1978 after seeing the Ramones play on *Don Kirshner's Rock Concert*, and later formed the Robins, releasing a record in 1980. Da Slyme, from St. John's, Newfoundland, were writing original songs by 1977 and put out a spray-paint-decorated LP in 1980. In Halifax, punk bands like Agro and Nobody's Heroes lined up to play at the Grafton Street Cafe, a rare venue that allowed musicians outside of the rather un-punk Atlantic Federation of Musicians to perform. The isolation of small-town Cape Breton bred the Dry Heeves, who released a series of experimental punk tapes before finally performing a show in 1984. And in Fredericton, a label owner named Peter Rowan helped the Vogons put out the city's first punk album after he started a local festival in the mid-'80s that finally cross-pollinated the region's various municipal punk scenes. While this is hardly a full account of early east-coast punk — many bands never recorded, making scenes tough to fully document — it's clear that the genre's rise gave musicians in the region a sense of possibility and self-sufficiency.

Outside of punk, one of the first alternative bands in Atlantic Canada to properly record their music was Null Set, a group of Nova Scotia College of Art and Design (NSCAD) students. They released a seven-inch EP, the Talking Heads–esque *New Job*, in 1980. For the most part, though, the early days of east-coast alternative was confined to concerts. Almost all live music was local, since the 10-plus hour trek from Montreal prevented most touring bands from heading to the region. In those early days, it felt like "a very isolated place," says Allison Outhit, who played in the new-wave band Staja/TANZ, and is now a vice-president of FACTOR, a music-funding body in Toronto. "You felt far away from everything."

Midway through the decade, the outside world began to creep in. In 1984, on invitation from NSCAD, a young New York band named Sonic Youth came to speak to a class and play the art school's cafeteria. Guitarist Thurston Moore said they played to "maybe eight people" — there was a big hardcore show across town, which some remember was headlined by Vancouver punks D.O.A. — but the Sonic Youth show left enough of an impression that it's widely considered a crucial chapter in the city's music history. Outhit, who was there, still calls it "a mind-blowing event for everybody concerned."

One of the Halifax scene's biggest early boosters was

Greg Clark, who opened Backstreet Amusements arcade in 1980. "All the punk kids started hanging out there," says Clark. And the punk kids wanted shows. So, seeing a business opportunity when the Grafton Street Cafe closed, Clark opened Club Flamingo in 1983 and started putting on all-ages concerts. It was only open a few months before the building was sold and the club shut down, but Clark continued to book music — and still does to this day.

In 1986, when a new iteration of Club Flamingo opened on Gottingen Street, its Halloween debut doubled as a release party for the compilation album *Out of the Fog: The Halifax Underground 1986*. The record was the first full-length document of the local alternative scene. Its release was more than just symbolic — the authors of the Canadian music tome *Have Not Been the Same* call the record proof to Haligonians that "alternative music could be made in their own backyard." Local band Jellyfishbabies dropped their self-titled debut album that same year, giving them a chance to tour and earning them kudos from the BBC's John Peel. They were the first band in the Halifax alternative scene to put out their own full-length, and, soon, the first to move away. The band released their second album from Toronto. "It just seemed like that's what it would take to have a career playing music — to move to a bigger centre and hook up with people who were willing to give everything up to play music," says Mike Belitsky, who joined the band after the move and now drums for the Sadies. Returning to Halifax was never really on his mind. "I'm just one of those people who feels like they have to be at the source, as opposed to starting the source," he says. After another lineup change and a move to New York, Jellyfishbabies disbanded.

Basic English, who appeared on *Out of the Fog* alongside Jellyfishbabies, also attempted a move to Toronto only to break up. But there was another band on the compilation who did gain traction: the October Game, whose vocalist, Sarah McLachlan, handled ticketing at Club Flamingo. Aside from the Jellyfishbabies and Basic English, "nobody was trying to make it in the music biz," says longtime scene-watcher Stephen Cooke, who covers Nova Scotia music for the Halifax *Chronicle-Herald*. "That wasn't really a concept until one of the guys from Nettwerk happened to spot Sarah McLachlan with her band."

When Greg Clark promoted a show for Vancouver band Moev in spring 1986, the October Game opened. Mark Jowett, a partner at Moev's label, Nettwerk, was in the audience and soon spearheaded a year-long push to sign McLachlan. It worked. McLachlan's success "started to help us out," Clark says. "All of a sudden, people were like, 'You can actually make money from this?'" says Cooke. McLachlan moved to British Columbia, where the label is headquartered, but back in Halifax, the ball was in motion: getting signed on the east coast was suddenly a real possibility. "Prior to that time, unless you were a fiddle player or Rita MacNeil, nobody had any kind of a career while still living in Halifax," Cooke says.

Most of the other bands that emerged around this time didn't last long, but many of their members went on to form or join more familiar acts. Few of them committed much to record. "It was expensive and it took a lot of money to put a record out, and not a lot of bands were doing it," says Sloan's Jay Ferguson. But these bands built a scene from the ground up, laying the foundation for what was to come. The cast of characters that emerged in the late '80s would become major players a few years later. Sloan's Patrick Pentland and Thrush Hermit drummer Cliff Gibb formed Happy Co., while future Joel Plaskett Emergency mainstay Dave Marsh helmed the band No Damn Fears with members of Jale and Sloan. And John Wesley Chisholm's Black Pool featured, over time, Chris Murphy of Sloan, Matt Murphy of the Super Friendz, and both Marsh and Tim Brennan of the Emergency.

In 1987, Jay Ferguson and Chris Murphy began jamming with their friend Henri Sangalang, forming the band Kearney Lake Rd. The riff-rock band made a few tapes and got the attention of Fredericton's Peter Rowan, who ran DTK Records. "When we started DTK, Halifax was a million miles away," Rowan says. "These little communities were creating music without any idea that 100 miles down the road, people were doing the same thing." Rowan took Kearney Lake Rd. on tour to Toronto and helped them record an album that was never released; they broke up in 1990. Rowan later managed Sloan, Eric's Trip, and the Hardship Post, and he co-founded the Halifax Pop Explosion music festival with Greg Clark in 1993.

Ferguson and Murphy joined Andrew Scott and Patrick Pentland to form Sloan in early 1991. The experienced musicians earned attention quickly. They landed a slot at the East Coast Music Awards — a rarity for an alternative band at the time — and when a rep from MCA Canada, who'd come on Ferguson's invitation, saw the band, he immediately wanted to discuss a contract. Rowan pushed MCA for a U.S. deal, and its newly acquired subsidiary Geffen came knocking. The band became the first in the region's alternative community to ride music-industry hype to a major-label contract while staying in Halifax. They also became the first major recorded band — aside from traditional and Celtic-influenced acts — to eagerly incorporate east-coast localisms into their lexicon. Most famously, Murphy's song "Underwhelmed," which helped earn the band its major-label interest, references "the LC," local slang for the province-run liquor store.

The band put out its full-length debut *Smeared* in 1992 through Geffen to much fanfare, only to be stonewalled by the label when their reference material shifted from Sonic Youth to the Beatles for its follow-up, *Twice Removed*. Geffen wasn't happy with the change and asked the band to re-record it. When they didn't, the label released the album anyway but gave it next to no support. Faced with the same possibility for all of their future records, the band decided to quietly break up. Sort of. It was a year-long, messy divorce that lasted most of 1995, spanning numerous awkward interviews and concerts, including a headlining gig at Edgefest at the Molson Canadian Amphitheatre in Toronto.

"We were just trying to avoid getting contractually fucked by Geffen, because if we said officially we were broken up, then we would be under a different set of rights than if we were an intact band that they dropped," Chris Murphy says. "So we didn't want to say that we were officially breaking up, and then what ended up happening was we ended up getting tons of press because of that." But there was also tension within the band's ranks, as drummer Andrew Scott

Some of the murderecords roster at a Stinkin' Rich seven-inch photoshoot, including Rob Benvie and Joel Plaskett of Thrush Hermit; "Stinkin' Rich" Terfry; Stephen Cooke; Ian McGettigan of Thrush Hermit; and Jay Ferguson and Patrick Pentland of Sloan. [© Catherine Stockhausen]

had moved to Toronto, making it impossible to practise. "I would rather break up than replace a member," says Murphy. "I would have rather started over."

IT WASN'T MUCH of a breakup. No one left or got replaced. Sloan was back in the studio recording *One Chord to Another* by Christmas 1995, and they fairly negotiated their way out of their Geffen contract soon after. But even if they had never gotten back together, the legacy of their first run was immeasurable. In a few short years, the band injected a huge sense of promise and possibility into Halifax and across the east coast. "That was a fun time," Cooke says. "Bands were

Chris Murphy at the murderecords office. [© Catherine Stockhausen]

really getting their shit together, learning how to write songs properly, and taking a little more of a professional attitude." Before Sloan, he says, "there wasn't a lot of ambition onstage. People were doing it for fun, and sometimes that's the right reason to do something, but once bands had to prove themselves a little bit more than that, the possibility of Halifax having some music worth remembering on a bigger scale finally came to fruition."

An indie-label ecosystem had blossomed. No Records, founded by future Halifax municipal councillor Waye Mason, emerged as a home for acts like the power-pop band Cool Blue Halo and hip-hop troupe Hip Club Groove. Cinnamon Toast Records put out albums by Outhit's new outfit Rebecca West and teenage band Plumtree. And, influenced by Ian MacKaye's Dischord Records in Washington,

D.C., Sloan decided to launch a label, too.

Backed by some of the band's Geffen funding, murderecords became a vehicle for creating a permanent document of their local scene, putting out a handful of albums and EPs and a slew of 45s. Left without a band for much of 1995, Murphy and Ferguson spent the year working out of the Barrington Street murderecords office, packaging records by hand and manually handling mail orders. The label's catalogue included releases from an east-coast who's who: the Super Friendz; Eric's Trip; Stinkin' Rich, now better known as Buck 65 or CBC Radio host Rich Terfry; and Kingston band the Inbreds, who later moved to Halifax themselves. "For so long, bands had been ignored in Halifax," Ferguson says. "It was such an especially fertile period in the early '90s. It was the right time to make sure everything was documented."

The glass ceiling that geography, economics, and history had long held over pop, rock, and alternative music in Atlantic Canada was, through Sloan, finally broken. Unlike their predecessors, from Hank Snow to Sarah McLachlan, Sloan managed to get a record deal without moving away, enlivening their own scene in the process. It was suddenly cool to be from the east coast — and, sometimes, to sing about it. Labels and journalists began to swarm the region, clamouring to discover the next Sloan. There were a few candidates, among them Eric's Trip, Jale, the Hardship Post, and Cool Blue Halo. One of the youngest contenders, a gang of kids from the Halifax suburb of Clayton Park, was called Thrush Hermit. The band had three constant members: Rob Benvie, Ian McGettigan, and Joel Plaskett.

HARBOUR BOYS

BILL PLASKETT AND Sharon MacDonald grew up on opposite sides of the Atlantic, but they met on the Pacific. Bill grew up in Dagenham, a London suburb, playing in traditional jazz and skiffle bands as a teen in the late '50s and early '60s. He went to university in Hull, in northern England, already versed in guitar, bass guitar, and tenor banjo. There, he grew obsessed with the early British folk revival, teaching himself to fingerpick and following the careers of the likes of Bert Jansch, John Renbourn, and Davy Graham. After graduating, Bill moved to Canada's west coast, spending his summers in the bush doing mining exploration and his winters slumming it in Vancouver, living in communal houses and teaching himself James Taylor songs. There, in 1968, he met Sharon MacDonald. She'd grown up in Halifax, studying ballet and character dancing, but had dropped out of Dalhousie University to move to British Columbia. After enrolling in Simon Fraser University in its early days, she realized that their only dance offerings were extra-curricular. She dropped out once again to join a group of like-minded Vancouverites teaching and dancing off-campus.

Mutual acquaintances introduced the two, and they became close, but just friends. They each moved away for a time — he to Pender Island, she to Europe, Africa, and Utah, where she studied at a repertory dance theatre. But Sharon and Bill reconnected at a Thanksgiving dinner in 1973 and became an item, marrying the next year. They talked about heading east, maybe to Montreal, but their van broke down before they got outside Vancouver. So they delivered vehicles across the country — first a station wagon to Quebec, then a half-ton truck to Cape Breton — which left them in Nova Scotia. Bill enrolled in a surveying course in the Annapolis Valley, and it was in the Valley town of Berwick, on April 18, 1975, that William Joel MacDonald Plaskett was born.

THE FAMILY MOVED around half a dozen times those first two years in Nova Scotia. Shortly after Joel was born, they settled near Lunenburg, on Nova Scotia's South Shore, where Bill put his new surveying skills to work and Sharon took a job at the local library. Their second child, Anna, was born four years later. The house was filled with music. Sharon would play Miles Davis, John Coltrane, Stevie Wonder — music she loved for dancing. Bill, meanwhile, had fallen hard for the British, Irish, and Scottish traditional folk revival after connecting with other musicians around Lunenburg. He helped start a coffee house called Out of the Woodwork

Joel Plaskett with his parents, Bill Plaskett and Sharon MacDonald.
[From Joel Plaskett's archives]

— named for the discovery, he says, of all these folk players suddenly coming out of nowhere. He formed a couple
of traditional bands, Starb'ard Side and Slum Gullion, and
eventually took so much of an interest in the scene that he
helped found the annual Lunenburg Folk Harbour Festival
in the mid-'80s. The Plaskett-MacDonald home played
host to the young festival's after-parties, and Bill recalls
that at one late-night gathering, acclaimed Newfoundland
fiddler Émile Benoit showed up; he parked himself in the
corner and fiddled and stomped so long he wore away the
oak floor's brand-new finish.

The young Joel was exposed to all of this, but it would
be decades before traditional folk influence seeped into his
music. At the time, he didn't think a whole lot of it. His lyrical sensibilities, though, developed early. "I always thought

that Joel's love of words comes from his love of nursery rhymes," Sharon says. "When he was two or three, I sang a lot of nursery rhymes to him. He knew hundreds of them — he just picked up on that stuff."

Bill offered to teach the boy guitar a few years later, but he wasn't interested. At 10, he tried the drums, but got bored. Next came the saxophone, which, Joel says, "didn't stick." He was digging the music he heard on the radio, though: the Four Tops, the Temptations, and — "probably because of *Back to the Future*" — Chuck Berry. He also grew obsessed with Billy Joel's *Glass Houses*, a record he brings up in interviews to this day. As he neared the end of elementary school, a new kid moved to town and built a half-pipe in his backyard, changing local youth culture forever. "He single-handedly pretty much brought punk rock and skateboarding to Lunenburg," Plaskett says. Skate culture vastly expanded his musical palette: Suicidal Tendencies, the Sex Pistols, Metallica. As the skinny pre-teen began his short skate career, he was getting his first real window into music written after John Bonham's death — and his first taste of the joy that comes from sharing music with like-minded people.

MIDWAY THROUGH THE '80s, Joel's mother, Sharon, decided to go back to school, enrolling at Mount Saint Vincent University in Halifax, about an hour's drive northeast. She commuted a day or two a week while still teaching dance in Lunenburg. But in 1987, as Joel was about to enter junior high, the family moved to the city. "I was ready to have a bit more happening — Lunenburg is beautiful, but it has some limitations," Sharon says. "There was no diversity. . . . I felt I wanted the kids to be more exposed to a broader spectrum of people." They settled near the university in the west-end suburb of Clayton Park. Early on, Sharon happened to run into Janet Benvie, an old friend from elementary school. It turned out that Janet had kids the same age as Joel and Anna, and they decided to introduce their children.

Plaskett met Rob Benvie for the first time that summer, before they each started grade seven at Clayton Park Junior High. Both of them remember the first few meetings as a bit cold. Plaskett didn't think he fit in with city kids; he says he felt like an "awkward kid from Lunenburg," while Benvie remembers being "kind of shy — it's always weird when your parents set you up with someone." Benvie introduced Plaskett to Ian McGettigan, another boy their age who'd moved to town from Newfoundland a few years earlier. He and Plaskett became fast friends, but it took a little longer for Benvie to warm up to the new kid. Still, he prepped the newcomer for the pressures of teenage life in the city, including the importance of name-brand clothes. "Rob warned him that there were a lot of people who were going to be concerned about branding," says McGettigan, who saw a kindred spirit in Plaskett. "Joel and I were coming at the social strata vortex of junior high — socioeconomic bullshit — from a similar angle." Plaskett assumed this meant surf-style brands like Ocean Pacific, but, McGettigan says, Benvie corrected him: "No, like Ralph Lauren." A few years later, the experience of adjusting to city-kid expectations snuck into Plaskett's lyrics for "The Great Pacific Ocean."

In the eighth grade, both Benvie and Plaskett decided to

pick up the guitar. Each insists the other learned first, influencing their own decision to play. Benvie and McGettigan had practised percussion in school, and when Benvie saw Bill Plaskett's collection of instruments, he started wondering how fun it could be to jam. The younger Plaskett finally asked his father for guitar lessons. "I liked music, but I saw it as an opportunity to hang out with my buddies," he says. "And then it took hold really fast."

Plaskett was finally receptive to his dad's folk teachings. The two soon banded together for what would be one of his first public performances, playing the intertwining guitars of Bert Jansch's "Angie" at a Harbour Folk Society show in town. "It was almost like that was the pinnacle of what I was able to teach Joel," Bill says. His son's interests were wandering elsewhere. "That was at the time he was also starting to spend hours under headphones in the basement, listening to Led Zeppelin."

The trio and other friends would have sleepovers to listen to CKDU, the college radio station out of Dalhousie, taping songs by local bands. They'd have Zeppelin seances, trying to summon the ghost of John Bonham. On weekends, they'd catch the bus downtown to buy records and look at guitars. Whatever iciness that remained from Plaskett and Benvie's first meeting, meanwhile, melted away as they began to play music together. On one weekend in 1989, the three decided to form a band, and, blank tape in hand, they recorded every sound they made. Benvie borrowed a drum kit from school, and McGettigan got a fretless bass from his mother's boyfriend. They called themselves Nabisco Fonzie — named, in part, after a *Happy Days*–themed compilation record Plaskett had called *Fonzie Favorites*. There was much goofing off, and McGettigan, whose absurd sense of humour later turned him into Thrush Hermit's comic foil, slipped into the role of early frontman. Music, Benvie says, "is how we bonded."*

Nabisco Fonzie gave them a taste of what it was like to make music, and soon enough, they decided it was time to start a real band. While the earlier project was all goof-offs and comedic jams, in their second iteration — as the Hoods — the friends took the craft more seriously. Through CKDU, they'd become inspired by the local music scene, going to as many all-ages shows downtown and at local universities as they could. "We were very, very into that, and quickly had aspirations to do that ourselves," Benvie says. "Joel and I both started writing songs. They weren't joke songs — they were super earnest."

Their friend Alex Grace had his own drum kit, and the trio invited him to join the band. The original members quickly realized two things: one, that they suddenly had to get organized and practise, and two, while the new drummer was "cool as hell," Benvie says, Grace wasn't very good behind the kit. But they kept him on board, and he helped deliver at least one major milestone for the band — their first concert, at the Shearwater Yacht Club across the Halifax harbour. Grace's brother helped set it up. It didn't go well. "It was a bunch of weird, rich, frat kinda guys who didn't really pay any attention," McGettigan says. Angry because their show sucked, the band stole an empty beer keg,

---

* Excerpts from the session, featuring at least one sexually suggestive request directed at a *Degrassi Junior High* character, can be heard on the "Embarrass Ourselves Awake" disc of Thrush Hermit's *Complete Recordings* box set.

The Hoods at their ninth-grade fashion show: Benvie, McGettigan, and Plaskett in front, with Alex Grace hidden behind the drum kit. [From Joel Plaskett's archives]

not realizing it served no value without its precious contents. They soldiered on, playing their ninth grade fashion show — in which Benvie and McGettigan also modelled — and a couple of dances, performing a handful of originals mixed with classic rock covers. By the end of junior high, though, it was over for Grace. The core trio wanted someone more devoted to the band. As he and Benvie split a pack of smokes at a communal party spot in the woods — some called it Ashtray Rock, but most just called it Ashtray — Benvie told Grace he was out.

Soon, too, came a new name. All classic rock fans, the members enjoyed '70s band names that were "cryptic, and maybe nonsensical, like Jethro Tull and Iron Butterfly,"

The Thrush Hermit high-school lineup: Ian McGettigan, Mike Catano, Joel Plaskett, and Rob Benvie. [From Joel Plaskett's archives]

Benvie says. He remembered hearing about a bird called the hermit thrush, but got the name backwards. And so the band became Thrush Hermit — to, eventually, mild regret. "People always called us the Thrush Hermits, which is a terrible name," he says. "Not that Thrush Hermit was that good. We were kind of doomed with that name."

As Plaskett, Benvie, and McGettigan started at Halifax West High School in 1990, their focus got more singular, and they deliberately tried to develop the reputation as The Guys in the Band. They recruited Mike Catano, whom McGettigan and Benvie had met during a percussion course, to be their drummer; he was a little young, but more dedicated than Grace had been. The band relocated jamming to Catano's parents' basement in Halifax's south end. By this time, Plaskett and Benvie were writing songs at a voracious pace, and after months of writing and practising, the band booked time to lay down their first real recordings. At Halifax's Centre for Art Tapes, the band helped paint the eight-track studio's walls in exchange for recording time. They recorded the pop-punky "This One's Mine," which appeared on the 1992 Halifax compilation *Hear and Now* alongside Sloan's "Underwhelmed."

The Hermit — their affectionate, preferred shorthand for the band — soon earned a few grand by recording a short-lived theme song for CBC-TV's *Street Cents*, a personal finance show aimed at teens, and even appeared on the show, where Plaskett explained their strategy for success: "We're completely prepared for a life of poverty." They used the cash to book more recording time. At Steve Comeau's Adinsound studio, they rounded out a collection of tracks that made up their first cassette release, *Nobody Famous*, including the song "Picturesque," which features young Plaskett shredding his heart out. "I would not enjoy listening to [the tape] now, other than as a nostalgia exercise," Benvie says. "I mean, it was slick — it shows kids who had a certain degree of sophistication — but it was very, very uncool, and sonically the songs were pretty bad." Plaskett cringes, too, preferring the Hoods' jokey basement tapes to the pro recordings: "As soon as you try and record bad music with a bit more fidelity, it gets a lot worse."*

---

*   Afraid of releasing the whole cassette to the masses, Plaskett and Benvie made only "This One's Mine" and "Picturesque" from *Nobody Famous* available on the 2010 Thrush Hermit box set. But curious fans can easily find the other tracks, "Tedious" and "The Topic Being," with a cursory Google search.

To make copies, the band would take the bus out to the Burnside industrial park across the Halifax harbour, where a local business let them hijack their multi-cassette deck for as long as they needed. They'd spend whole days there, dubbing four tapes at a time until they amassed dozens. "I distinctly remember us all walking home along the train tracks, *Stand by Me* style, with a big sack of cassettes we'd just made," McGettigan says. Together, with the help of Plaskett's family, the band would photocopy and cut out all the liner notes and package the tapes to sell at shows. And the shows? They were about to get bigger.

FOR A WHILE, Peter Rowan hosted an event called "Two Buck Tuesdays" at the Flamingo, hosting up-and-coming local bands for a pair of shows, one all ages, every Tuesday. Thrush Hermit approached him with a tape one summer, asking "Mr. Rowan" if they could play at one. It was the first time he'd been called that. "I thought, *who the hell are you talking to?*" Rowan says with a chuckle. He agreed to let them play.

The Hermit had spent two weeks earlier that summer at a local music shop's long-running "Summer Rock" camp, tightening their playing and learning how to put on a proper concert. Armed with these new skills, they saw Two Buck Tuesdays as their chance to prove their worth. To hype it up, the band smothered the city with posters and requested their tape on CKDU constantly. It worked — 199 people showed up, breaking the event's attendance record.

They played a mix of originals and covers, including, in the encore, KISS's "Strutter." The show, McGettigan remembers, was pretty amazing — at least "by Halifax standards." A few minutes after the encore, Plaskett ran into Sloan's Chris Murphy in the bathroom. He certainly knew about Sloan — he'd been to their second-ever show at Dalhousie University a few months earlier, and looked up to the band as captains of the local scene — and his memory of the conversation is crystal clear. "He said, 'Cool, you guys like KISS too? We should do a KISS tribute night.' And I was like, 'Yeah, awesome.'"* The men's-room meeting sparked a long friendship between the two and their bands, in spite of a seven-year age difference. "They were great to us, and a huge influence on all of us, no doubt, and on me," — especially, Plaskett says, "the lyricism."

Sloan's "Underwhelmed" was an important song for Plaskett. Not only was the Hermit cast in its original video, playing spin the bottle with a group of teenage girls, but it was Plaskett's first major introduction to local specificity in song. The key moment is actually an off-the-cuff reference: "She told me to loosen up on her way to the LC," Murphy sings, shouting out slang for the Nova Scotia Liquor Corporation's retail outlets. But it's a distinct enough localism that it came across as a revelation to the young songwriter, who still calls it one of his favourite lines ever. The influence would stretch throughout his whole career. "It was dawning on me that you can just write what you know," he

---

* Murphy followed through on his word: in December 1993, both bands were on the bill for a KISS tribute night aptly called KISSmas.

One of the posters for Thrush Hermit's debut Two Buck Tuesday, which introduced the band to much of the city.
[From Joel Plaskett's archives]

says. "You can mention things that other people might not know about, but if the song is great then they're going to want to learn about that." Of equal weight in this influence was Bruce Springsteen, who he started listening to around the same time. "The world of New Jersey he paints is really romanticized," Plaskett says. "Little towns where there's not a lot going on, but sound great in Bruce's songs."

Sloan's influence quickly seeped into Thrush Hermit's sound, and the unfortunate-but-brilliant nickname "Clone" became local parlance for the Hermit for a while, much to their chagrin. But they were certainly attentive students: in between Sloan's official releases, Plaskett and his bandmates would get a schoolmate, who had a sister in Jale, to sneak them copies of the band's four-track demos. It was no mistake, then, that Thrush Hermit's second tape, *John Boomer*, leaned far more toward Sloan's early fuzzy, hooky sound than *Nobody Famous*. "Sloan definitely blew the roof off the town," Plaskett says. "It was hard not to mimic them." Still, other influences came across on the tape's six tracks. "When you're a teenager, you love everything," Benvie says. "We wanted to have the live show of the Beastie Boys and the musical sense of Superchunk."

John Boomer came out in 1993, as Plaskett, Benvie, and McGettigan were in their final months of high school. They started playing more shows, but, tied to the day-to-day trappings of education, it was hard for Thrush Hermit to grow much creatively. They spent a lot of time driving around Halifax in Benvie's mom's Ford Tempo, talking about making music. "We would get in that car and drive around listening to *Physical Graffiti* or the Clash or the

Pixies," Plaskett says. "Just drive around Clayton Park or downtown. Maybe we'd go and have a coffee, and then we'd get back in the car and just drive. It was suburban. There was nothing to do."

As the end of high school approached for Plaskett, Benvie, and McGettigan, they started dreaming of touring life. But there was a hitch: Catano, a year younger than the rest of the band, wouldn't be able to go. His parents wouldn't let him. Realizing they needed a drummer who would commit as intensely as the rest of the band, the original three members decided to let him go. "I'm sure he was pissed," Plaskett says — with good reason, considering the band was about to become more serious than ever before.

When Plaskett's friend Melanie Rusinak found out Thrush Hermit needed a drummer, she suggested Cliff Gibb, who'd played in the power-pop band Cool Blue Halo. The three had jammed for fun before Catano left the Hermit, and the band liked Gibb's style. He was a few years older than the first three members, and even had a day job, which impressed the near-grads. ("I was an *adult*," he jokes.) He was quickly and warmly welcomed into the Hermit. Catano, meanwhile, kept playing music, eventually as part of North of America, and now lives in Chicago, where he's a renowned bicycle maker.

At the same time they were luring in a new drummer, a young woman named Angie Fenwick showed up on the scene, anxious to be a part of the business end of Halifax's burgeoning indie community. She connected with Peter Rowan and Chip Sutherland, who were managing up-and-coming east coast bands including Eric's Trip, the

Hardship Post, and Sloan. They, in turn, connected her with Chris Murphy. At the time, he happened to be helping local label Cinnamon Toast Records put out Thrush Hermit's *Ammo* seven-inch, featuring new songs "Pink Is the Colour" and "Cookie." When Murphy had to hit the road for a while, he got Fenwick to pick up where he left off, and the songs sparked enough of an interest that she decided to see the Hermit in concert. "They definitely had something special," Fenwick says. She talked to the band after the show, and they kept in touch. Within a few months, the Hermit asked her to manage them. The band began to play bars around town as much as they could, even though Fenwick had to fill out special request forms for the liquor board every time, and a parent — often Bill Plaskett, but sometimes Sharon MacDonald or Janet Benvie — had to chaperone them.

Other bands in the scene took pity on the teenagers. "Miniature" Tim Stewart, who played in the band Bubaiskull, remembers sneaking the Hermit beers between sets at Two Buck Tuesdays — except for young Plaskett, who was a staunch teetotaler. Even back then, Stewart says, Plaskett had an interminable focus. "I don't think there's a large percentage of people playing in bands at any given time who are really looking to make a sustainable career, especially from a young age," Stewart says. "I think Joel's one of those cats who's different that way. And he's managed to pull it off."

Before he could pull it off, though, his band had to get noticed.

PETER ROWAN REMEMBERS the phone call well. It was August 1992, and Joyce Linehan, who worked for Sub Pop, wanted to know if Sloan was signed. He explained that Geffen had already nabbed them. Since Linehan had to go to Nova Scotia anyway to visit family, she asked if any shows were going on that she might want to see. "Oh yeah," Rowan told her. "There's a great show this Saturday." He hung up and immediately called Greg Clark to make good on his bluff. They cobbled together a triple-bill of buzzy east-coast bands to play at Clark's latest bar, the Double Deuce, that Saturday: Bubaiskull, Eric's Trip, and Tag, who later morphed into Jale.

It was a pivotal concert for alternative music in Atlantic Canada. Sub Pop went on to sign Eric's Trip, Jale, and the Hardship Post, featuring the first two on the scene-showcasing compilation EP *Never Mind the Molluscs*. Reviewing the EP in March 1993, *Melody Maker*'s Everett True brazenly declared Halifax the "New Seattle," and soon went to Halifax to profile Sloan and Jale. By the end of 1993, the Seattle comparison showed up in publications like the *New York Times Magazine* and the British *Independent* newspaper. As Lisa Simpson once said, "Anything that's the something of the something isn't really the anything of anything," and the Seattle metaphor became a source of regular frustration. "It was a bit of a drag at the time," Jay Ferguson says, as he and others regularly defended the city's sense of individuality. Mike Campbell, who chronicled the east coast for MuchMusic for much of the '90s, calls it a "backhanded compliment that no one took seriously." The hype, though, certainly helped. "Our scene wouldn't have exploded if Sub

The poster for Greg Clark and Peter Rowan's last-minute concert that got Sub Pop interested in the east coast. [Designed by Adam Cavill]

Pop hadn't shown up at the perfect moment in time," Rowan says. "We were basically anointed by God." It was certainly a boon for bands like the Hardship Post, who'd moved to Halifax from St. John's, Newfoundland. "Sub Pop gave us the chance to do more than we would have otherwise," says the band's frontman, Sebastian Lippa.

More than 20 years later, *Melody Maker*'s True regrets his choice of words. "It was a pretty damn bad way to pigeonhole (and pretend there was) a coherent 'scene,'" he says. Having been one of the first international journalists to discover Nirvana and bring grunge to the world's attention, True was under pressure to work his magic again. "It was sort of a piss-take of the fact that post–Sub Pop and Nirvana, everyone was looking to create a 'New Seattle' fucking city in America. They all seemed like nice kids, but it was an absurd title to give something that had very little indeed to do with Seattle or grunge."*

In early 1993, fresh off the *Melody Maker* story, a freelance writer named Brad Gooch pitched a story to *Harper's Bazaar* on Seattle scene "spinoff" cities, and Halifax was at the top of the pile. Despite contending against Chapel Hill, North Carolina — home to Superchunk and their growing label, Merge Records — and the buzzing music centre of Austin, Texas, Halifax got the green light from Gooch's editor. He flew up, saw a show at the Double Deuce, and talked to bands and fans. The story features both Sloan and Jale, though it's unclear how much he really knew

---

* True also lost the cassette tape of his Sloan interview and invented quotes for print — "something the band never quite forgave me for."

about Sloan when he wrote it; while he interviewed Chris Murphy inside the Double Deuce, he identified him only as the ex-frontman of Black Pool. The feature caps off with an interview with the youngest of the city's hyped bands, Thrush Hermit, who managed to pivot their discussion with Gooch from the Halifax "sound" to an ironic dissection of skateboard culture and hipness in Lunenburg.

Gooch took a liking to the Hermit, who gave him a copy of the *John Boomer* tape. That tape changed a few hands, and copies were likely made. Within a month or two, a copy wound up on the desk of Clyde Lieberman, a former career songwriter who'd just moved to New York to run BMG Music Publishing's east-coast artists and repertoire team. Talent scouting was a new gig for him, and he was trying to figure out the ins and outs when, through Gooch and others, he heard about the buzz coming out of Halifax. The Thrush Hermit tape was enough to convince him to buy a ticket to Nova Scotia.

The day he landed, Lieberman went straight to the Double Deuce to watch the Hermit play and immediately realized he was not wasting his time. Benvie's new song, "French Inhale," blew him away. And by then, Plaskett had grown to tower above most people, giving him a commanding stage presence — Lieberman couldn't keep his eyes off him. "I was witnessing exactly what you look for when you love music," Lieberman says. "These were guys who had respect for the greats, but they were blazing their own trail. And I was absolutely, 100 percent convinced that as soon as I discovered Joel Plaskett that I had discovered a star. When you do A&R for a living, that's your dream come true."

He told Fenwick he wanted to sign the band and went back to New York to plead Thrush Hermit's case to his bosses. BMG bit, and the band signed a developmental publishing deal before their June graduation. It was standard fare for a young group. In exchange for a share of their publishing rights — the intellectual property rights behind their compositions, like lyrics and melody — BMG gave the band a modest advance while letting them keep the rights to the recordings proper. That kept the door open for a more lucrative recording deal down the road. BMG, in other words, was investing in growth: seeing the Hermit's potential, they offered a cash injection to give the band the time and money to hone their craft, hoping for a payout when the Hermit made it big. Fresh out of high school, that's what the band needed — a chance to focus on writing and practising while they were still young, without the hit-making pressure that comes with a major-label deal. All they had to do was make good on the investment.

WAITING TO BE DISCOVERED

IT'S 1995, AND Jason Lee is badgering Shannen Doherty as she shops for a denim jacket. "What kills me about you is your inability to function on the same plane of existence as the rest of us," Doherty's character, Rene, tells Lee's Brodie in the Kevin Smith film *Mallrats*. "Okay, okay. I see you want to continue with this charade of ending our union," Lee says. And so he begins to set out terms for how they'll split their things, including visitation rights for the mall he loves. As they argue, a teenaged voice sings a pop-punk anthem that echoes Brodie's abrasiveness: "Don't coming looking for me. I'll come looking for you."

The voice belongs to Joel Plaskett, in his silver-screen debut, singing Thrush Hermit's "Hated It" to the band's biggest audience yet. The *Mallrats* soundtrack was a pretty good fit for the Hermit: a record aimed at slackers and skaters, featuring the music of Weezer, Sublime, and Silverchair. Scoring Kevin Smith's follow-up to the critically acclaimed

Clerks was good exposure for the band, who were shopping for a label, and it put a couple of bucks in their pocket. But *Mallrats*, whose soundtrack sold a few thousand copies, was not the first option presented to the band. No, that was *Dumb and Dumber*, the 1994 Jim Carrey and Jeff Daniels blockbuster whose soundtrack went Gold, selling more than 500,000 copies. It would have netted the band thousands of dollars in royalties, paying off for years, as reruns aired on TV. Their reason for turning it down was simple, says bassist Ian McGettigan: "In our eyes, Jim Carrey wasn't cool."

This was the attitude that defined Thrush Hermit's career. "We had reservations about the slick music industry. Even though we sounded like Superchunk, we admired Fugazi," says Rob Benvie. They were trying to attract labels but kept a DIY attitude, often to the hindrance of their careers — or at least their bank account. But they never looked back. "It was our way or the highway," McGettigan says. Whether for a soundtrack deal, a record producer, or a frontman, the band would never compromise. On one hand, that garnered the Hermit credibility and music-industry attention. On the other, it helped fuel the band's eventual collapse, in spite of all the promise they showed in 1993.

THE BMG DEAL injected serious confidence into the band, and Plaskett, Benvie, and McGettigan made a pact to put off university to try to get the Hermit off the ground. Plaskett's parents supported Joel's pursuit of music over higher education. For Bill, the would-be high-school skiffle star, it was a chance to see his son live the dream he didn't. Sharon didn't hesitate, either. "I remember a lot of people saying to me, 'Aren't you worried he'll never go back?'" she says. "And I said, 'I'd be a real hypocrite, because I was a '60s university dropout.'"

From then on, the members' every gesture and decision had the band in mind. Plaskett used one of Benvie's lyrics from "Cookie" as his yearbook grad photo caption.* McGettigan, who was the lead in his high school's production of *Grease* that year, turned down a well-paying job at a local dinner theatre, much to his mother's chagrin. Their lives were deeply intertwined so, naturally, they spent a lot of time together — Fenwick and Gibb most of all. Both a couple years older than the rest of the band, they found themselves socializing away from the others, who couldn't actually get into bars, and soon started secretly dating. When the drummer told his bandmates, they just laughed. They'd already figured it out. "You can't keep secrets in Halifax," Fenwick says.

Gibb blurted out the news before the Hermit's first tour, since, with Fenwick coming along, he figured it would become obvious. The band had planned to take Gibb's car for a quick jaunt to Montreal and back, but there was a hitch. Shortly before the trip, while he and Sloan's Patrick Pentland were hanging out with Fenwick at her Barrington Street apartment, Gibb heard a sickening crunch come from the street. "I looked out, and it was my car," he says.

---

* That lyric was "I will hunt you down tomorrow," which, after more than 20 years of reflection, Plaskett very much regrets.

"The whole front end was crushed, and I saw a truck taking off." He ran into the street in his sock feet and chased the truck. After disappearing for a bit, the vehicle circled back with a different driver. "It wasn't the same guy, so obviously, somebody was drunk," Gibb says. The truck's owner offered to pay for the damage in cash, but the band needed a car as soon as possible to leave for the tour. So the stranger paid for a rental, too. And the five of them — Fenwick included — piled into a rented sedan, with all their gear in a pod on top, to drive to Montreal.

The cramped ride "was miserable, but it was really fun," Benvie says. Playing to a handful of people in Montreal, the notably tall Joel jumped on the stage and hit his head on the ceiling mid-song. "He just went with it," Gibb says. "He rolled around the ground in agony, but played it up as a move." It was a fun taste of what was to come. The band soon bought a van with their BMG money, and later that summer hit the road again opening for the Hardship Post.

Sloan, riding the high of their Geffen contract, had taken to bringing local bands they were fans of to support them on tour. That fall, they brought Thrush Hermit to open a handful of university shows. "That was fairly mind-blowing," McGettigan says. "We were playing these college shows for 900, 1,200 people. The energy was really a lot." Sloan wanted the band to make the full west-coast trek with them, but the Hermit crew balked, worried they'd lose too much money.* But even on the worst days, playing

---

* They still made up to $1,000 a night from merch sales. And on these first tours, a very boyish-looking Benvie was in charge of depositing the money — up to $10,000 at a time — to frequently confused bank tellers.

shows on the road blew the young band away. "We were all so new and wide-eyed; we could sell five cassettes and think it was a great day," says Mike Nelson, who sold merch for the Hermit on that tour and went on to manage Sloan. That first taste of big gigs "was when it really all came together," McGettigan says.

When the tour stopped at Concordia University in Montreal, the members of a West Island band named Local Rabbits came to see them play. They were a year younger than Thrush Hermit and felt a connection as soon as the Halifax band hit the stage — especially when they covered Bryan Adams's "One Night Love Affair." Singer-guitarist Peter Elkas was floored. "Musical irony was not as present as it is today — you wouldn't have a band doing wacky covers very often," he says. The Rabbits snuck backstage after the show to meet the band and formed a quick, if strange, bond. Elkas likens the experience to "bizarro *Seinfeld*" — each band member had an eerily similar counterpart in the other band. As an anglo group from the suburb of a French city in a French province, the Rabbits didn't feel very connected to their own local scene, but with the Hermit, they found an instant kinship. They began regularly touring and goofing off together, and Elkas and his Rabbits bandmates remain friends with the members of the Hermit to this day.

On another early Hermit tour, Rich Terfry — the hip-hop artist now known as Buck 65 — came along as tour manager. After one particularly long drive, the band pulled into a strip mall parking lot to stretch and promptly locked their keys in the van. Things quickly got worse: the shop behind the van caught fire, and they couldn't move the vehicle when the fire department showed up, forcing officials to work around it. Then, awkwardly, the band asked the firefighters if they could use their tools to break into the van. "Deeply ashamed, we sat and watched as half a dozen of Montreal's finest worked the vehicle's every crack and crevice," recounts Terfry in his 2015 book, *Wicked and Weird.* "After struggling valiantly for 10 minutes, they gave up." Then, only after the fire crew had left, McGettigan broke the lock himself.

LABELS BEGAN TO circle Thrush Hermit after the BMG deal, but the band staved them off as they developed their sound, trying to cling to their indie-rock mentality. "We saw the music industry as populated by clowns — as it is," Benvie says. Instead, they unleashed a series of independent releases. They'd already put out the *Ammo* seven-inch through Cinnamon Toast Records. They also found a fan in Randy Kaye, an A&R rep for Slash Records from California, who put out a seven-inch of *John Boomer* tracks on his own boutique label, Genius. And Sloan, in their newfound roles as Halifax scene incubators, wanted to put out a proper Thrush Hermit release, too.

Later that fall, the elder band set up a room at Halifax's Pier 21 to demo the songs that would make up their sophomore album *Twice Removed*, and invited the Hermit to record in their space. Brenndan McGuire, who had done sound on the Sloan-Hermit tour, came in to record it. There were difficulties — "it was freezing and a ridiculous place to record," Jay Ferguson says — but the late 1993 sessions turned into *Smart Bomb*, a seven-song EP of mostly new material that became Thrush Hermit's first major statement in the marketplace.

It's a fuzzy, nostalgic record whose pace rarely slows down, opening with the one-two punch of Plaskett's zeitgeist-perfect "Hated It" and Benvie's pop-punk "French Inhale." While later Thrush Hermit material found Plaskett as rock populist and Benvie as skronky auteur, here, the nascent songwriters' material was similar. While making *Smart Bomb*, the band members took likings to different parts of the writing and recording process. McGettigan turned his attention to sounds, tones, and album artwork — all habits he'd keep for the long term. Plaskett and Benvie, meanwhile, found themselves lingering on lyrics. "We would actively talk about words and why they mattered," Plaskett says. "Rob was a guy I learned a great deal from, lyrically. He's a writer — he could always dazzle with words. He could strike the mix of humour and patheticness in his songs. I still think about Rob's tunes and how much they influenced me." "Hated It" touches upon a theme that runs through much of Plaskett's later work — though, at the time, it was unintentional. What Plaskett sings in the chorus is now a familiar refrain within his catalogue: "All my friends have left me / to go to other cities." But, at the time of *Smart Bomb*, there hadn't been any Halifax exodus to speak of; McGettigan and Benvie were his best friends, and his mentors in Sloan were still in town. It's "a real train-of-thought song," Plaskett says. He'd revisit the notion of being left behind much more consciously a decade later.

THE FIRST HALF of 1994 was slow for the Hermit. Plaskett, Benvie, and McGettigan still aimlessly drove around Halifax, listening to music and charting out plans for the band, often until 4 a.m. even though McGettigan had to show up for shifts at Mark's Work Wearhouse most mornings. Unlike the others, the bassist was straddling two worlds. While Benvie and Plaskett still lived at home, he lived on his own, and the day jobs paid for his apartment. McGettigan was also, for a time, an "Aroma Ranger" on the Halifax waterfront, handing out free coffee from a tank strapped to his back while wearing a safari outfit. When they weren't driving around, the three friends still made music. Sometimes it was under the guise of the Tim Robbins Experience, a blithe, irreverent hardcore/new-wavey project that let Plaskett, Benvie, and McGettigan stray from their usual instruments — and sensibility. Plaskett, meanwhile, would talk about music for hours to anyone who'd listen. Angie Fenwick and Peter Elkas recall many phone calls that went late into the night, and Chris Murphy dreaded getting rides home to his family's place in Clayton Park with Plaskett after concerts downtown: "I knew I would probably have to spend an hour and a half talking about music in the car with him," he says. But Murphy looks back at it a little more fondly now. "He's become iconic, and I got all this one-on-one time with him when he was younger. He was so young and just talking in my parents' driveway for so long. It was romantic."

Smart Bomb was released in May 1994, and it necessitated promotion, so the band decided to make a music video. Benvie's woozy "French Inhale," a three-and-a-half-minute fan favourite, became the candidate. With the help of an arts grant, they hired Laura Crapo, also known as Laura Borealis, to direct. Crapo, a recent NSCAD grad who'd studied video and performance art, filmed the project in June at the Khyber Centre for the Arts on Barrington Street. Half the video showcases the band in wild makeup playing erratically against an all-pink backdrop, while the other half follows stoned teenagers making out, goofing off, and biting each other. To do the makeup, Crapo flew in Rebecca Kraatz, a friend from Victoria, British Columbia, who was studying makeup artistry in Toronto. Plaskett struck up a conversation with Kraatz as she dolled him up for the shoot, and he was smitten: "I was like, *And who are you?* I just remember being really enamoured with her." Kraatz had a boyfriend at the time, but, she says, "I remember thinking Joel was funny, and really kind." They clicked, and, for kicks, she drew a fake bruise on Plaskett's face when the shoot was done. He drove her to the airport for her flight back to Toronto; on the way, they talked about her car — a '65 Beaumont — and the old instrumental songs she loved, like Santo & Johnny's "Sleepwalk."

Kraatz broke up with her boyfriend a few weeks later, eventually striking up a long-distance relationship with Plaskett. The "French Inhale" shoot turned out to be a particularly romantic one. Crapo and Benvie soon dated for a time, and Fenwick and Gibb got engaged — they're still married.

Plaskett and Angie Fenwick Gibb, circa 1994. [© Cliff Fenwick Gibb]

THE BAND SPENT the rest of the year on the road and recording with alt-rock tastemakers. Beck had signed a similar developmental deal with BMG Publishing a few years earlier, releasing his breakthrough album, *Mellow Gold*, in 1994. That July, Clyde Lieberman enlisted two of that album's producers, Rob Schnapf and Tom Rothrock, to record with the Hermit at Dreamland Studios in Woodstock, N.Y. Two songs, both Plaskett's, emerged as singles from this session. The first, the summery pop tune "Take Another Drag," came out as a single on Schnapf and Rothrock's Bong Load Custom Records, backed by an early version of *Sweet Homewrecker*'s "Came and Went." The other Woodstock standout, "Glum Boy," is pure Pavement. Trade Plaskett's high pitch for Stephen Malkmus's baritone, and it'd fit right in on *Slanted and Enchanted*. It showed up as the C-side of the *French Inhale* double seven-inch that California fan Randy Kaye put out on his boutique label, Genius; the band's signatures are etched into the D-side.

When she was called to direct the "French Inhale" video, Crapo was living in Chicago, where she'd briefly dated Steve Albini. The acclaimed *In Utero*, *Surfer Rosa*, and *No Pocky for Kitty* producer-engineer had just started the band Shellac, and Crapo brought an advance copy of their first album with her to the shoot. The Hermit gobbled it up — Cliff Fenwick Gibb, in particular, was a huge fan of Albini's earlier work in Big Black — and they mused about how cool it'd be to record with him. Unexpectedly, Crapo offered to ask him about it, and, after showing him one of the band's early seven-inches, Albini was game.

The band stopped in Chicago on one of their early U.S. tours in November 1994. Albini's studio was in his house, and he was still in bed when the Hermit arrived, so they drove around the city until he woke up. Albini, whose style is more hands-off engineer than sound-sculpting producer, worked efficiently. He recorded seven songs for the band over a single weekend but offered very little feedback. Occasionally, he was blunt. "Sounds pretty good. Maybe try singing this time," he instructed once. At best, he was vague. When McGettigan recorded the vocals for "Every Morning I Reread the Postcards," he offered unclear instructions: "Do the Billy Ocean bit." Behind Albini's cold exterior, though, was an absurd sense of humour. When the band first showed up, they could only find the recording booth, but not the control room. In the living room, meanwhile, there was a huge painting of a nude woman. When Albini

pressed the woman's nipple, a bookshelf moved, revealing a
secret staircase to the control room in the attic.

Albini was also a strict businessman. He demanded his
fee from the band as soon as they finished recording. The
band had expected him to invoice them, so they didn't have
enough money on hand; they had to ask Crapo to cover it.
Still, the Hermit got the last laugh, Cliff says: they didn't
tell Albini they were going to release the recordings and got
away with paying the cheaper demo rate.

The Hermit released most of the Albini recordings as
The Great Pacific Ocean EP, and they marked a clear shift
away from Sloan's influence. Like *Smart Bomb*, it's nostalgic
in tone, but this time with a twist of melancholy — Plaskett,
Benvie, and McGettigan sing of widening distances and
disappearing. There are straightforward, poppier songs,
including "Claim to Lame," that move the band's sound
consciously in the direction of Superchunk. Meanwhile,
Plaskett's "The Great Pacific Ocean" and Benvie's "Patriot"
play with the tension and release the band had succeeded
with on "Hated It." Murderecords released the EP as a CD,
but the band got it into their heads that they wanted to put
out a picture-disc vinyl. They got a small American label to
co-fund the project, half-and-half. When the band found
a manufacturer to press the vinyl, though, it turned out the
company wasn't used to doing picture discs and boxed them
without letting them fully set, warping nearly every one.

"A lot of them simply wouldn't play," Benvie says. "We
had put a deposit down for them and simply said, 'We're
not going to pay the rest of the money.' So they ended up
actually being kind of cheap, but useless." The band sold the

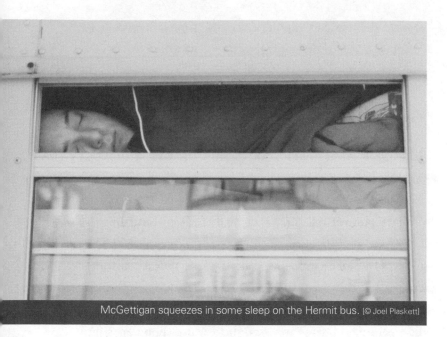

McGettigan squeezes in some sleep on the Hermit bus. [© Joel Plaskett]

discs for a buck apiece at one point. "It was one of the many adventures that we had where we spent a lot of money on idiotic, ambitious projects, for a band that had no money."

The band toured the EP supporting the likes of Urge Overkill and Guided by Voices. The *New York Times* took immediate notice of the Hermit's wistful nostalgia at a show in New York City, pointing out that their "smudging pop-rock songs" had "a recurring obsession: high schoolers' separation anxiety."

By then, the band was accustomed to the road. Lieberman's connections earned them a few perks that helped them on the long drives. During one of the Hermit's trips to New York, he was excited to show them one of his other recent discoveries: the Wu-Tang Clan, whom he'd recently helped sign a similar publishing deal. He gave them a pre-release cassette of *Enter the Wu-Tang (36 Chambers)*, and it became a regular Hermit highway soundtrack. And they found other ways to stay entertained: after abandoning their first van, an '83 Econoline, in a Gottingen Street parking lot — where a homeless man later lived in it — they bought a short school bus from a dealer in Saint John, New Brunswick, and retrofitted it to hold gear and five bunks. Each bunk had its own name and comfort level: The Tomb, The Shits, The Comf, The Snakepit, and The Upper Bowl. The Local Rabbits toured in the same model of school bus, and their designs became a source of great competition — Peter Elkas claims the Rabbits' bus incorporated an entire king-sized bed.

With a place to sleep, the band didn't need to worry about overspending. "We took great pride in never losing money on tour, even when we were making nothing," Benvie says. "If we were getting $100 for the show, we slept in the bus that night. Even though our music wasn't very punk rock, and our lifestyle wasn't very punk rock, we had a bit of a punk rock attitude toward making our band work."

THE SLOW BUILD of the Hermit's career had afforded them plenty of opportunity by 1995, but their publishing advance from BMG was running out. If the band was going to keep going, they needed to finally sign with a label. The timing wasn't great — the hype around Halifax was waning, diminishing the Hermit's star power. Other bands had begun to dissolve, and Sloan's members were slinking away to Ontario. By the start of the year, the media had begun referring to the city's Seattle-like hype in the past tense, invoking the same nostalgia as the Hermit's early releases. And while the Hermit were associating with power players through Lieberman, they weren't getting any closer to signing a record deal.

Not that the band always had their best financial interests in mind. "We definitely had our asses up in the indie-cred world at the time," says McGettigan. Turning down the *Dumb and Dumber* soundtrack was a particularly brash move. "It would have changed our lives," the bassist says, "but we said no." They self-sabotaged far more publicly at the 1995 Edgefest music festival in Toronto. It was billed as Sloan's final concert and featured much of the murderecords roster; the label even released a compilation EP for the show that featured its bands covering each other. The crowd at the Molson Canadian Amphitheatre was the biggest Thrush Hermit had ever played for — close to 7,000 people — giving them a real chance to make a name for themselves.

Instead, in what the *Montreal Gazette* called a "stroke of genius," they spent their entire set playing Steve Miller Band songs. "We were always super cheeky and thought the whole summer festival thing was a bit ridiculous," McGettigan says. Still, the stunt did not go over well with the promoter, or with Chris Murphy, who helped get the Hermit onto the bill. "In my mind, it was a missed opportunity to show how good they were," Murphy says. But he got over himself by the end of the set, joining the Hermit and a slew of interlopers, including the Local Rabbits, for the grand finale of "Take the Money and Run."

The Hermit had been making their way to California

regularly by this point, playing shows at influential L.A. clubs like Jabberjaw and Whisky a Go Go. They had earned a fan in Joe Fleischer, editor of the music industry magazine *HITS* and a conduit of influence for major labels. Clyde Lieberman had tipped him off to the band, and he began writing about them frequently in his column and pointing labels in their direction. Through a family friend, he also helped get the band on the *Mallrats* soundtrack. "There was a lot of excitement about the band, and a lot of the majors turned out to see them," Fleischer says. He spent a lot of time talking with the members about what directions they could take, educating them on the pros and cons of major labels — and encouraging them to never, ever compromise their sound for radio, even if a label pushed them to.

They found another champion in Randy Kaye. He'd put out two of their seven-inches by then on his boutique label, Genius, but his day job was doing A&R for the venerable punk imprint Slash Records. He wanted to sign the Hermit to Slash and even got label owner Bob Biggs to take the boys to a shooting range in L.A. "He rented us a Glock and the *Dirty Harry* revolver — like, the giant revolver," Plaskett says. "I was the first guy to shoot it, and I remember feeling it in my shoulder the next day."

Behind the scenes in the Hermit camp, though, there was some hesitation toward Slash. The whole team loved Randy Kaye, says manager Angie Fenwick Gibb. But Slash was a smaller label and wouldn't have given the band much money to help them grow — especially at the pace Lieberman's bosses at BMG Music Publishing wanted for the band it had invested in. Kaye's clout in the music industry was actually growing, and he was plotting a move to Warner Bros. That would have been ideal for the band, but the timing simply didn't work out. Kaye needed at least six months to make the move and set something in motion, but between their publisher's demands and their own wallets, the Hermit team was sandwiched with pressure and couldn't wait. "He was heartbroken. I was heartbroken," Angie says. "It was a matter of looking for the right situation. And unfortunately, the right situation didn't present itself at the right time." Kaye died in 2006.

Not all was lost. Darren Johnson, a fresh-faced A&R rep with Elektra Records, had been skulking around Halifax for a while and took notice of the Hermit. It was the Hardship Post that first turned Johnson on to the scene, and he was all but ready to make that band a major-label offer when he found out they were breaking up. He'd taken notice of Sloan, too, and hoped to move in once they dissolved their first major-label contract with Geffen. By the time both of those ventures fell through, though, he'd spent enough time around Halifax to take an interest in the Hermit. They'd opened for both bands enough over the course of Johnson's efforts that he realized he'd found another gem. He thought the Hermit had a phenomenal live show, but he had private worries that the band might be more limited in studio. "The question was always whether that magic could be captured in a recording — and actually translate outside of the visual experience of seeing Joel doing his amazing lead-singer, lead-guitar thing," Johnson says. "The other guys were a good presence live, as well."

Seymour Stein had recently started at Elektra and, with

Johnson's nudging, had taken an interest in the Hermit, too. A punk pioneer who'd signed the Ramones, the Talking Heads, and Madonna, Stein carried enough clout to convince Sylvia Rhone, the label's chief executive, to take a chance with the band, Johnson says. Lieberman pressed other labels to look at the Hermit, and a few tried wining and dining them, but Johnson was the only one to come back with a concrete offer to fund a whole album. At first, the band was wary: Johnson came across as a little quiet and reserved, and it turned a few of them off. But he was persistent, says Cliff: "I changed my tune when I got to know him."

It was now 1996, three years after the band had signed their developmental deal with BMG, and they badly needed a cash injection. In New York, Angie remembers, Lieberman's team was pushing the band to sign with anyone who'd bring them a good return on their investment. When Johnson promised the Hermit they'd be his number-one priority at Elektra, they got on board. Luckily, says Angie, the team "made sure we had a good buyout clause."

THEY INKED THE Elektra deal at Halifax's Five Fishermen restaurant. As a gesture to show his clout, Johnson brought along Stein, who regaled the Hermit with stories. He'd lunched with Brian Wilson the week before, he told a quiet Plaskett, and went on a tirade about the Beach Boys co-founder's melody writing. "Meanwhile, Seymour had potatoes on his nose," Plaskett says with a laugh. "But he was a super engaging, awesome storyteller."

The record deal netted the band a few hundred grand to live off — and with it, a mandate to deliver Elektra a full-length debut. Lieberman and Angie soon generated a list of potential producers. Butch Vig, Steve Miller, and Ric Ocasek all came up. During one Halifax Pop Explosion festival, Everclear's Art Alexakis — who'd earlier wanted to sign them to Capitol — even showed up to plead his case to produce them. But under a mainstream producer, the Hermit feared they'd be tampered with. Radio at the time was flooded with macho-style grunge bands like Alice in Chains and Soundgarden, who bored the Hermit, and they had no desire to trade their sound or cred for dollars. After listening to piles and piles of records, trying to hone in on a production style they liked, the band put in their own request: Doug Easley. Fresh off recording Pavement's *Wowee Zowee*, Easley had also worked with the Grifters and Guided by Voices, and the Hermit wanted his stamp on their full-length debut. Being a hot new band on a major label had its perks. What the band wanted, the band got. They headed down to Easley's studio in Memphis.

Over six weeks, the band hammered out the songs that would make up *Sweet Homewrecker*, taking time off here and there to soak in the Tennessee sun, devour southern barbecue, and go bowling. By this point, they'd become known for their powerful live show — channelling the energy of Led Zeppelin and the Steve Miller Band, shredding whenever their short pop songs would allow, and doing it all in front of an enormous neon sign that read "ROCK & ROLL." McGettigan — proprietor of the neon sign — had even begun to wrap the headstock of his bass with tissue paper,

McGettigan didn't just play — he performed. [From Joel Plaskett's archives]

light it on fire, and spit grain alcohol on it, sending a fire-ball into the air. But while recording, they were a different band. After seeing the Hermit's "crazy" live show, Easley was surprised at what he saw in the studio. "They were just sort of conservative," he says in a southern drawl. "They didn't want to go out on any limb." When Johnson stopped by to check in on the recording, he noticed the same thing: "There was an *oomph* that just felt like it was missing from some of the riffs."

Homewrecker's overall sound fits somewhere along the Weezer-Superchunk continuum, possessing a distinctly '90s alternative aura, but a sense of uncertainty hangs over it that the band now acknowledges. Even the guitars' trademark fuzz is all but gone. "It's kind of a sprawling, unfocused statement," McGettigan says. Plaskett calls the Memphis recording experience "amazing," but says, "We couldn't really wing it. Everything was scripted." The Hermit was a band restrained, wondering what it was supposed to do under pressure from a record company. At the time, Benvie said, "I think we found our own sound." But soon after it was done, they found the material hard to play live. What they really wanted, Benvie says now, was "to jam more and make things more band-oriented."

Part of the identity crisis was related to the band's divergent songwriting styles. By the *Homewrecker* sessions, Plaskett's songs leaned more heavily toward pop-rock, while Benvie's were becoming less accessible. The teenaged squeak that permeated Plaskett's earlier recordings was all but gone from his voice, and he laced pop flavour with a melancholy aftertaste on songs like "I'm Sorry If Your Heart Has No More Room." Benvie took a different direction, playing with jangly ups and downs on songs like "Noosed and Haloed Swear Words," while his track "Snubbed" veered into post-punk. McGettigan's sole contribution, meanwhile, was its own separate beast. If his neon rock & roll sign wasn't enough of an indication, "On the Sneak" was a harbinger of the hard-rock sound the band would later come to lean on.

Johnson thought the different styles accomplished a necessary balancing act. "It still sounded like the same band," he says, "but they kept it from being one-dimensional." In the end, the record erred on the side of Plaskett's poptimism, featuring eight of his songs versus five of Benvie's. "Joel's charismatic and good-looking, and I think they really wanted to make him the front guy, but it left me feeling a little full of angst," Benvie says. He started to worry where exactly he fit in the band. But, like Sloan, the Hermit operated as a democracy and made decisions that favoured the group over any one member. Since they were already skeptical of major labels, they decided to subvert Elektra's expectations, fading Plaskett into the background whenever they could. Even when the label released Plaskett's "North Dakota" as a single, the band didn't make a video for it — choosing, instead, to film one for McGettigan's "On the Sneak."

THRUSH HERMIT RETURNED to Halifax after recording *Sweet Homewrecker* to face another major-label reality — incessant delays. For the most part, the band had moved at a steady clip since high school, recording material, releasing it, and playing shows to support it. But for the rest of 1996, they mostly laid low as they waited for the right moment to release *Sweet Homewrecker* with full support from Elektra.

Now that they had a regular stream of income, they rented a space at the corner of Gottingen and Cornwallis

Streets to practise and record. Half the band had driven to Nashville during the Memphis *Homewrecker* sessions, and there they'd bought an Otari 8-track tape machine to make demos. It became a practice-space mainstay. Making music, after all, was their job; as Plaskett says, "We'd go to work every day." There, Thrush Hermit recorded a seven-inch for murderecords, featuring Benvie's "Giddy with the Drugs" backed with Plaskett's "The Ugly Details." It would be the label's last release for the former Sloan Clones, severing the final official tie with their elder mentors. With the Elektra contract, the Hermit finally had a clear, separate identity.

"That was sort of sad for me," Chris Murphy says. But by then, the members of Sloan were going through their own set of changes. By the time they released 1996's *One Chord to Another*, the heady days of murderecords' community documenting were winding down. Sloan's return as a band also heralded another transition for its members: to Toronto, away from the scene they'd helped build. Drummer Andrew Scott had moved there in 1993, breeding tension within the band as the remaining three Haligonians watched the kids come up from behind. "Part of the frustration I felt when he was gone was that we weren't rehearsing, and bands like Hardship Post, I was really jealous of," Murphy says. "They were so fucking *good*. And I was like, *Fuck, we suck*. And we really did."

But it wasn't music that made Sloan move — they'd already made a statement years earlier by signing to a major and staying at home. When they pulled the trigger, Murphy admits, it was "mostly for girls," as each member found themselves partners with someone who worked, or wanted to work, in Toronto. The move, he concedes, did help the band. "It's easier to do our job here. We could have probably stayed, but it's a pain in the ass to live in different places."

One by one, the members all moved to Canada's biggest city: first Scott, then Murphy and Jay Ferguson in 1997, followed by Patrick Pentland the next year. The move should have been jarring for Murphy, who found himself frustrated when bands like Jellyfishbabies left for Ontario's allegedly greener pastures. In the end, it wasn't jarring at all. "I moved with a bit of a shrug, even though it was part of Sloan's cachet that we were from out there." But, he says, "I think we haven't had that kind of cachet ever since we left."

With Sloan gone, Thrush Hermit had an opportunity to carry the torch as Halifax's major-label hometown heroes. And McGettigan insists that after this, the tides of influence started moving in the other direction, as Sloan's songs — most notably Patrick Pentland's, like "Money City Maniacs" from *Navy Blues* — got crunchy again. "God knows they definitely influenced us and gave us everything in the beginning," McGettigan says. By the late '90s, though, "it was a little bit reciprocal."

As Sloan left, they unknowingly took what was left of the industry's east-coast hype with them, and the Hermit would go on to borrow a few more things from the elder band's narrative: dashed dreams, clashing egos, and brash decisions.

SNUBBED

SWEET HOMEWRECKER WAS finally released in February 1997, and the Hermit set out to tour the U.S. What followed was a series of events that left them — to borrow a word from Sloan — underwhelmed. Just days after Elektra released "North Dakota" as a single, the band got a call from the label on their clunky bag phone somewhere along some U.S. highway. It was bad news: the single, and the album, weren't going to get any label support.

Cliff Fenwick Gibb remembers it being Darren Johnson on the call, but Johnson thinks the label would have gone over his head to break the news. No matter the messenger, it sent the Hermit into a rut they spent a long time digging out of. With no promotion and lacklustre distribution behind *Homewrecker*'s release, the tour floundered. Their shows were virtually empty. "We played all over the place," Cliff remembers, "but it'd be like playing during lunch hour at some sports pub."

Long tours often meant trouble for the Hermit's vehicles. Cliff Fenwick Gibb was usually called upon to solve the problem.
[© Joel Plaskett]

The record, Johnson says, "didn't fit into any neat box." There was no narrative, grand or grassroots, for Elektra to exploit. Without a clear radio-pop hit, the marketing and promotions teams shied away from *Sweet Homewrecker*. Geography, too, came into play. The Hermit lacked the notoriety that their alternative Atlantic Canadian predecessors had, like being anointed by Sub Pop; there was neither a familiar narrative nor place of origin for the U.S. media and major-label machine to attach to the band. To leverage indie success in the pre-blog age, Johnson says, "you really had to be talked about in a handful of magazines, and that just wasn't going on."

Within Elektra, turmoil was lurking by the time of *Sweet Homewrecker*'s release: Seymour Stein, Thrush Hermit's champion in theory, was on his way out, while Johnson, their champion in practice, wielded next to no power at the company. The label's dollars and energy were being spent elsewhere. Third Eye Blind, among other bands, got an Elektra deal at the same time as Thrush Hermit and spent 1997 riding the high of radio-friendly hits like "Semi-Charmed Life." Johnson, whose recruiting efforts for Elektra skewed away from that kind of prefab pop, is still frustrated about *Homewrecker*'s fate.* "The problem with *Sweet Homewrecker*," he says, "is that it's too good of an album — for people whose whole life is built on appealing to the masses — to really take the time to appreciate and understand."

Because they were signed to a U.S. label, Canada was just a footnote for the Elektra-planned album cycle, and they returned to smaller shows at home, too. *Homewrecker* got a bit, but not much, national press; in a very quick blurb, the *Toronto Star* hailed its "sense of honest fun and big guitar-riffing bubbles." The Hermit felt cut adrift, says Benvie. "Bands that we were friends with back home, who were more focused on Canada, just kind of seemed to be getting more done while we were beating our heads against the wall." Steve Jordan, who did A&R for Warner Music Canada at the time and later founded the Polaris Music Prize, remembers the band playing to a half-empty Horseshoe Tavern after *Homewrecker*'s release. Jordan campaigned for his label — technically Elektra's Canadian counterpart — to grab a stake in the Hermit deal, but he got no traction. "If an artist

---

* While at Elektra, he also worked with a Chicago post-hardcore band named Trenchmouth, whose drummer was Fred Armisen — a future star of *Saturday Night Live* and *Portlandia*.

was signed directly to a U.S. label," Jordan says, "especially if it was something developing, it was less likely to have that kind of push behind it in its home territory."

The label upheaval that left *Sweet Homewrecker* stagnant and the band playing to half-filled rooms only got worse as 1997 rolled along. In quick succession, Elektra dropped the Hermit and fired Darren Johnson — likely, Johnson says, because neither party was delivering hits. In the previous decade, major labels had been willing to invest in artists for the longer term, letting those whose first records weren't smash hits, such as U2, develop over time. By the mid-'90s, that was done; majors were hungry for alternative hits in the wake of Nirvana, and their patience was thin. Behind the scenes, too, changes were happening that would soon burst the alt-rock bubble. In 1996, the United States deregulated its radio industry, leading to the amalgamation of huge station chains that cared more about boosting ratings than careful sonic curation. The alternative sound that grunge brought to the fore didn't bring in as many listeners as pop, shifting industry priorities. So it was becoming increasingly common for labels to give up on alternative bands before giving them a chance to show their potential; just a year after Elektra cut ties with Thrush Hermit, in fact, they dropped the Austin, Texas, band Spoon, who'd later sign with Merge and become one of the most enduring indie bands of the early 20th century.

After Johnson was sacked, no one in the Hermit ever heard from him again. Angie Fenwick Gibb heard he'd been escorted out of the building; he hadn't been, but he kept a distance from the bands he signed to make a clean break from the music industry. "I just followed their career from afar after that," he says. He's now an intellectual property lawyer in New York.

"When the news came, we weren't really very broken up about it," Angie says. The label, she thought, wasn't doing anything the band couldn't do on its own. Luckily, their lawyer — Ken Anderson, whose roster of clients also included the Beastie Boys — had negotiated a five-figure buyout clause. "If Elektra wanted to dump the band, they had to pay us," Angie says, "so we took the money and ran."

On the road, the Hermit started refocusing their efforts — sometimes abandoning them altogether. Four months after *Homewrecker* came out, the band set up for a gig in Norman, Oklahoma, and decided not to bother loading their neon rock & roll sign into the club. "We were bored out of our skulls, and the shows had been sucking," Plaskett says. In front of a tiny crowd, the band mostly played B-sides and new songs, largely without a care. After the show, he says, Tyson Meade of the alt-rock band Chainsaw Kittens came up and said hello. Regret set in. "I remember it dawning on us that these guys are musicians, and maybe we should be playing to impress them," Plaskett says. Then Meade introduced him to some of his friends in the audience. One of them, it turned out, was the Flaming Lips' Wayne Coyne. The regret deepened. "Of all the bands in the U.S. who would appreciate a neon rock & roll sign," Plaskett says, "those were the guys we didn't set it up for."

Later, at Flashbacks Nite Club in Kelowna, British Columbia, the Hermit was in the middle of playing the new song "We Are Being Reduced" when the show's promoter approached the stage with a request for something more upbeat, hoping to bring the 30-odd people at the back of the room closer to the front: "Pick it up, we're dying in here." As if that wasn't insulting enough, after the show, someone from the audience came over as the Hermit loaded their gear into the school bus and asked politely if they were the band. "Yeah," one of them said. The man changed gears: "Well, you fuckin' sucked." The compounding insults stuck in Plaskett's mind. A few years later, he decided to pay Kelowna back the best way he could — through song, on *La De Da*'s "I Love This Town." In it, he explicitly, though sarcastically, references Kelowna as the only town he hates — even though Kraatz's family is from there. "That song," he says, "gets me heat in my family."

The band fell into some odd habits while touring *Homewrecker*. Plaskett spent the entire tour in uniform, alternating between all-green and all-blue utility shirt-and-pants combos that looked like a gas station attendant's outfit, sealed with a gold "JOEL" beltbuckle given to him by Kraatz. They'd let McGettigan scream his way through "Jailhouse Rock" onstage. And to squeeze some fun out of the sparsely attended shows, the Hermit began to fill their concerts with shredding and jamming, moving away from *Homewrecker*'s conservatism. "We would go berserk," McGettigan says, even "when there would just be the sound man there" — but living up to their long-haired, classic rock–loving stereotypes, the sound guys always loved it. The band, Plaskett especially, started rediscovering their own classic- and riff-rock roots, spending time on the road listening to Black Sabbath and Cactus. "We were finally having fun again after stuff that was really scripted," Plaskett says. "It was getting more sprawling."

DURING DOWNTIME IN Halifax, the Hermit kept jamming. "We had awhile there where we were paralyzed and couldn't release anything or do anything, but we were still practising all the time," Benvie says. They also started trying new things, some of which were more creative than others. Everyone in the band — except for Plaskett — invested in a "nice little scoot": a '78 Pontiac Phoenix for McGettigan to drive in a stock car race. On the advice of Kraatz's father, Plaskett instead went out west and bought a car of his own: a green '69 Pontiac Parisienne. McGettigan began using the Hermit's rehearsal space to record other local bands, including a side project he and Benvie joined called Rick of the Skins. Plaskett fell in with a different crowd of musicians, too, including Charles Austin and Drew Yamada of the Super Friendz, "Miniature" Tim Stewart from Bubaiskull, and Andrew Glencross; he began drumming with them in 1998 in the avant-rock band Neuseiland.

Plaskett also started to fool around with a pedal steel guitar he'd bought in Memphis and was trying his hand at recording songs on his own. He and Kraatz were still dating long-distance — while she'd tried to move to Halifax twice, it was hard to find work in the city. Still, she was largely responsible for widening Plaskett's musical palette beyond the realm of rock. "Her musical tastes are great and not affected by any trends," he says. She turned Plaskett on to music from the '50s, much of which leaned toward country:

Lefty Frizzell, George Jones, Bo Diddley, the Delmore Brothers. "Every once in a while she hears something modern and likes it, and it has nothing to do with whether it's hip or cool — she doesn't pay attention to any of that."

Armed with these old-school influences — and some more contemporary ones, including Vic Chesnutt — Plaskett began writing songs that wouldn't fit anywhere in Thrush Hermit's catalogue. By 1998, he'd recorded an album's worth of such material. The songs were distinctly moodier than Thrush Hermit's — where the occasional vague heartbreak of the band's early output was expressed through outward-looking nostalgia, these tracks turned that sadness inwards. Cobbled together, Plaskett admits, these first solo songs made for "kind of a depressing record."

The collection's mood was fuelled by the death of his grandfather, Dr. Robert MacDonald, in 1996. Plaskett's mother, Sharon MacDonald, believes he inherited much of his positive, forward-thinking personality from Dr. MacDonald, whom he called Pa. Plaskett left a tour a few days early to be there for the funeral, where he was struck by a phrase someone used to eulogize his grandfather: "A gentle man of God." His death was tough on Plaskett during an already tough year, thanks to all the uncertainty that came from signing with Elektra. It influenced much of the material, from the recurring doctor character and the words from the eulogy, which appear in "Goodbye, Doctor," to the title Plaskett later gave the album: *In Need of Medical Attention*. To voice the fictional doctor on the record, Plaskett turned to another older man he respected: Al Tuck, his friend and mentor. Tuck, a prolific songwriter whose catalogue runs deep but is not as widely known as Plaskett's, jokes that the guest spot continues to pay: "If I'm out in B.C. doing a show with no publicity, and the only two people who show up are there because they know me as the doctor on Joel's album, that's a practical favour, really."

After wrapping up recording, Plaskett mixed the songs with Rick White, of Eric's Trip and Elevator, in Moncton. Kraatz, who moved to Halifax for good later in 1998, supplied the artwork. It would be a year before *Medical Attention* came out, though. Thrush Hermit, as always, took precedence for Plaskett. Angie recalls meeting him for lunch after she heard the recordings. "I remember saying, 'This is something I could really do something with — what do you want to do with it?'" she says. His response? "Nothing. I'm in Thrush Hermit. And that's the direction that I'll keep going in."

IT TOOK A while for the Hermit to work out the terms of their buyout with Elektra, so they just kept on practising. By the summer of '98, they'd cleared the paperwork and worked out enough new tracks to fill an album. After everything that had happened with Elektra, they decided to finance it themselves. "We had nothing to lose at that point, in a way," McGettigan says. "We weren't going to try to make a really big, American statement. But we still had enough money that we could afford to do whatever we wanted to do."

The Hermit went to Gas Station Recording in Toronto's Liberty Village to make the record with producer Dale Morningstar. For a month, they stayed at McGettigan's

Plaskett at Gas Station studio during the recording of *Clayton Park*.
[From Joel Plaskett's archives]

mother's house north of the city, driving in every day in a motorhome they'd bought from Sloan to take on tour. They recorded a track a day for two weeks, overdubbed for another week, and mixed for a fourth. Morningstar took a liking to the Nova Scotian boys as they bonded over early '70s Stones and other classic rock cuts. He'd only ever heard the Hermit once before — on the demos they'd sent him — and came to the sessions without any expectation of what they'd be like. "I was really struck by how Joel and the other guys had their act together," he says. "They let me do my thing, but they had a really good vision for the album." At night, the band would drive the motorhome around the then-industrial neighbourhood, sometimes with Morningstar and McGettigan lying on the roof. They also offered the vehicle as part of their payment for the sessions; Morningstar politely declined.

The record became *Clayton Park*. On it, the Hermit's guitar fuzz is back, but it's more "Communication Breakdown" than Dinosaur Jr. The album is a return to the Hermit's roots — literally, in its name, and sonically, in its reverence for the classic rock the members were raised on. One writer called it a "balls-out rock 'n' roll extravaganza." The *Toronto Star* loved it, calling it deserving of a Juno, though its critic worried the record was a few years (or decades) behind the riff-rock zeitgeist. More than 15 years after its release, it can be safely said that the record was a few years ahead of its time, too, as artists like Jack White and the Black Keys have since ushered in a new era of classic-rock revival. After an album spent waffling over label expectations, it was a bold statement about who they were and where they were from. "It's the record on which Joel said, 'I'm a Canadian, I'm from eastern Canada, and I'm damn proud of it,'" says Clyde Lieberman, who upholds *Clayton Park* as the Hermit's best work.

The major-label pressure to produce a frontman was gone, but Plaskett by then had undeniably emerged as bandleader. The Hermit cut 11 songs for the final record, but only two Benvie songs appear — "Headin' South" and "Western Dreamz." McGettigan, the Harrison to their lopsided Lennon-McCartney, squeezed in a single song, "(Oh Man) What to Do." They also recorded a cover of Budgie's "Nude Disintegrating Parachutist Woman" that wound up on the cutting-room floor.

Lyrically, Plaskett toys with themes many of his songs are known for today — leaving and travelling — while trading *Sweet Homewrecker*'s American-heavy references for Canadiana. He watches someone walk away in "Before You Leave," but hits the road on his own in "The Day We Hit the Coast." The most dramatic travelling song here, though, is Benvie's. It may be Plaskett singing about wilted realities of allegedly greener pastures at the start of "Western Dreamz," but they're his bandmate's words. Understandably, he still cites Benvie as a chief lyrical influence.

The Hermit's slump over the previous few years had been especially tough for Cliff, who was closer to his 30s than the rest of the band. To pass time on the road, he'd been reading computer programming books for fun. He'd never gone to school for it, however, and didn't think he'd be able to turn programming into a job. But as they were recording *Clayton Park*, a legitimate opportunity came up at a local telecom company — and he flew to Halifax for an interview. To his surprise, he was offered the job shortly after flying back to Toronto to finish the record. He decided he couldn't turn down the opportunity. "I still loved playing every single night, but I had enough of the touring, and being away from my wife," he says. Cliff told the band he had to quit when the record was done. They were devastated. "That was a real blow," McGettigan says. They weren't just losing a beloved bandmate; they were losing him after making the record they'd always wanted to make with him.

But they didn't have time to mope. Too excited about the album to slow down, the Hermit immediately started looking for a new drummer. They settled on Halifax mainstay Benn Ross, who'd previously played with the Super Friendz's Matt Murphy and had actually replaced Cliff in a

Plaskett, Benvie, McGettigan, and new Thrush Hermit drummer Benn Ross. [© Ingram Barss]

previous band called Weasel Faced Judge. "We had to really put him through the ringer," Benvie says. "Not only did we have to learn this new album, but he had to learn all our old songs, and we're one of those bands who like to write a different set list every night."

Ross expected he'd just be filling in for a few gigs, but he was welcomed as an official member. "It was a pleasure to play with a band who had experience playing bigger shows, and they had their stuff organized compared to a lot of folks locally at the time," he says. But he was an introverted guy and had a hard time fitting in with the three original Hermit members, who'd by then been friends for more than a decade. "They all had the same sense of humour and social energy, so I just kept to myself and focused on playing."

At the same time, Angie Fenwick Gibb's health had been in decline, and she started working from home — both managing Thrush Hermit and running the Halifax Pop Explosion festival, then called Halifax on Music. After a while, she couldn't keep up and had to hand back the Hermit's reins. She and the band were heartbroken — but, again, the Hermit had to focus their energy on the road ahead. Left with another huge hole to fill, they tapped murderecords managing director Colin Mackenzie, who also happened to be McGettigan's roommate, to take the wheel in Angie's stead. The band had lost some blood, but they managed to bandage their wounds. At least for a little while.

WITH A NEW record in the can, rumours spread that Thrush Hermit would spend the summer of 1998 in L.A. meeting "important people." There were talks of courting another label, but the band didn't want to make another slickly produced album when they were happy recording in their own jam space. Instead, the members went their separate ways for a while and let *Clayton Park* go unreleased for the time being. "It felt like there was a real change coming," McGettigan says. He and Benvie took a trip to Europe in the fall of '98, leaving Plaskett behind. Plaskett had plenty to do on his own, though. He finally left Clayton Park — the place — moving in with Kraatz downtown. And with a few months until *Clayton Park* — the record — was coming out, he began rehearsing his *Medical Attention* songs with a five-piece band, including Neuseiland bandmates Charles Austin and Andrew Glencross, Tracy Stevens, and veteran

Halifax drummer Dave Marsh.

Once 1999 kicked off, the Hermit got back into the swing of things. Before Angie left the band, she'd struck a deal with Hamilton indie label Sonic Unyon to release *Clayton Park*, and it came out that spring to much acclaim. With a renewed focus on Canada, the band started drawing bigger audiences as they began touring, though sometimes this was due to strange pairings on concert bills — like a show in Saint John, New Brunswick, with Alanis Morissette and Crash Test Dummies. The band's aesthetic for the record, they decreed, was "decidedly au naturale," and they grew out their hair and showcased the jams and winding solos that had long made up their live shows. Plaskett, whose songs were the face of the album, also became the face of the band in concert. He took centre stage and, for the first time, would occasionally ditch his guitar, going full frontman for tracks like "From the Back of the Film." This freed him up to play around onstage; he'd carry lighting rigs to blast the crowd or bring audience members onstage for a mock game of *Who Wants to Be a Millionaire* during "Film."

The new approach pushed the rest of the band to the side, and it left fellow songwriter Benvie worried about his place in the Hermit. "Joel really stepped up and really wanted to be the leader," he says. "Which, at the time, I was freaked out by, because he had a really strong vision, and I didn't really know what I wanted to do." Plaskett's dominance on *Clayton Park* was frustrating enough, but as the band prepped material for what would have been its follow-up, the creative dynamic shifted even further out of Benvie's favour.

"I was resenting Joel a little bit. But it sort of made sense, for an outside observer. Joel's a very charismatic showman, and his songs were more accessible and commercial, and we'd made some videos where he was the star, and he looked really great. I'm not sure Ian had so much angst about it, but I personally was like, *I don't know where I fit in this band anymore.* And it just hit me, like, *Why couldn't you leave the band?* Even though we'd grown up together, maybe it'd just ended.

"So I quit."

THRUSH HERMIT'S SPLIT was amicable, but certainly unpleasant. "It wasn't like we were at each other's throats, but I think Rob was unhappy. It was an awkward time," Plaskett says. He talked things over with McGettigan — who had long served as the comic foil whenever tensions rose between his bandmates — and they agreed that there was no Thrush Hermit without Benvie. The band, they realized, was over.

A host of other factors were at play, too. The band's Elektra buyout money was drying up. And they were still only playing for a few hundred people a night — a respectable number but not enough to pay the bills forever. With *Clayton Park*, the band had "done its statement," McGettigan says. "There was no common ground left, in a way." Looking back, Angie Fenwick Gibb thinks the dominoes may have started to fall once she and Cliff left. "I feel pretty strongly that there's a certain magic between these four guys — between the five of us, or the six of us including Clyde. When you start to break apart those pieces,

The original five-piece Emergency at the CMJ festival in New York: Tracy Stevens, Plaskett, Dave Marsh, Andrew Glencross, and Charles Austin. [From Joel Plaskett's archives]

sometimes you just can't make the whole be what it needs to be anymore. And there's no way to foresee that before it actually happens."

The Hermit announced their split on September 21, 1999. The breakup announcement coincided with the release of *In Need of Medical Attention* on Minneapolis's No Alternative Records. Not to be confused with the Halifax-based No Records, No Alternative was run by Kim Randall, now a music supervisor in Los Angeles, who'd met the band when they toured through the Twin Cities. By eschewing the Hermit's regular business connections and releasing with No Alternative, Plaskett was able to distribute and market his solo music as its own product — a move entirely beneficial in wake of the band's breakup. Though the close timing of *Medical Attention*'s release and the Hermit's breakup was pure chance, a new album needs tour support, and it was quickly followed by Plaskett's first solo shows with the five-piece backing band. They performed just a handful of times, including at a Barrington Street deli that September and a pair in New York for the CMJ music festival. The Canadian press didn't pay much attention to the record upon its release; the only mention *Medical Attention* received in the *Toronto Star*, for instance, was in a passing comment made by Plaskett's mother in a story about a lecture she gave on Nova Scotian textile history. ("I'm quite fond of it," she said.) There was at least some ink in the international music press, though. The British magazine *New Musical Express* went to one CMJ show, calling Plaskett "a star," comparing his banter to Wayne Coyne and likening his songs to Big Star's.

His solo career showed promise right out of the gate, but, just like his time in Thrush Hermit, there were complications. Years of constant touring had taken its toll on Plaskett. The frail frontman would catch colds on the road all the time, sometimes singing through throat infections — even though he largely shunned the hard-partying rock 'n' roll lifestyle, barely drinking and never smoking. That fall, his health caught up with him. Feeling run down, he got some bloodwork done to see what was up. When a month passed with no answer — "they screwed up," Plaskett says — he visited his doctor again.

The results had come in. "Your white count's really low," Plaskett recalls the doctor saying.

"What do you mean really low?"

"Well, really low. It *could* be leukemia, but we have to get to the bottom of why it's low."

This was an unexpected response. "Well, I'm about to go on tour."

"Oh, I wouldn't recommend that," the doctor said. "If your count is still this low — mind you these results are a few weeks old — if you catch a cold, it could get worse. You could die."

That never happened, clearly, but the conversation illustrated the risks regular touring were putting on Plaskett's well-being. Further examinations were ordered, including a bone marrow test that meant a painful marrow extraction from the hip. His white blood-cell count at the time was fluctuating, he says, "but we never really got to the bottom of it." He eventually stopped eating wheat — his mother is celiac, but he'd never been diagnosed — which dramatically improved his immune system. But right then, slowing down was his first priority.*

He called the rest of the band, who were about to leave for the Front Man War Tour with their friends in the Local Rabbits and the Flashing Lights, Matt Murphy's new band. Making matters worse, it was supposed to double as their farewell tour. "It was really weird, because it kinda came out of nowhere for everyone," Plaskett says. "And Rob, I remember, was really angry. I think he just wanted the thing to end."

The Hermit bailed on the full tour, instead playing just a handful of dates in December, with stops across Ontario and Quebec. Interviewed before the Toronto stop, Plaskett said he wanted the band to be remembered as "Thinkers. We sometimes overthought things, but we were always thinking,

---

*   *In Need of Medical Attention* came out just as Plaskett announced he was
     sick, but the album name was a pure — if eerie — coincidence.

and sometimes the thinking worked against us, and sometimes it worked for us, but I think a lot of bands just don't think." They were just a little cult band, he said — not that big, just doing stuff for fun. Then, after a long pause: "I hope we're remembered by someone."

BY THE END of 1999, most of the bands who sparked the east-coast pop explosion had burned out. Mike Campbell, host of MuchMusic's east-coast showcase *MuchEast*, watched so many of his favourite bands break up that he'd regularly host "wake" episodes from a graveyard, complete with band T-shirts over tombstones. The lure of labels brought in an injection of cash that gave more opportunities to the local music scene than ever before, but in the long term, the deals bands were offered were rarely lucrative. It was also a scene that, in its isolation, was built on bands playing for each other. "Everybody was happy to just play for their peers," Peter Rowan says. The pressure to do more than that — without much potential to earn more — took its toll on the city and the region, and a scene that might have flourished in isolation instead collapsed in on itself.

"Once you start touring, suddenly you realize, *huh, this isn't exactly what I want to do*," says Colin Mackenzie, who was murderecords' managing director. The Hardship Post lost their drummer and toured as a two-piece to the surprise and despair of fans, breaking up soon after. Eric's Trip, whose music was often fuelled by the relationship of members Julie Doiron and Rick White, slowly lost momentum after that relationship ended — though both of them went on to prolific recording careers of their own, and they remained friendly, keeping the doors open for the occasional reunion. Two of Jale's members left, and while former Jellyfishbaby Mike Belitsky was enlisted to flesh out the band, it was dropped by Sub Pop in 1997, along with much of the label's Canadian roster. The Super Friendz broke up in 1997, and guitarist Matt Murphy headed to Ontario, eventually forming the Flashing Lights. Cool Blue Halo split in the middle of a major-label bidding war in 1998. Plumtree, the band behind the comic-inspiring song "Scott Pilgrim" and one of the last of the "New Seattle" acts to hang on, broke up by mid-2000 as its members scattered around the world.

The Trews, who'd formed in Antigonish, Nova Scotia in the late '90s, left for Ontario in 2001 rather than try to make it in Halifax first. "There was still a lot of that '90s hangover left," says guitarist John Angus MacDonald. The east coast went through a transition period, but there was a sense the scene was clinging to the past. "The afterglow of the heyday still had Halifax captured, and we didn't fit that trend at all."

It was a "crazy arc," says Super Friendz bassist Charles Austin. "People were getting signed, getting a lot of money, and then getting dropped, and just ending up with nothing. The thing about all those Halifax bands — with the exception of Sloan — was when they ended, it was basically like you didn't have anything to show for five years of your life. Other than *hey, you were in that cool band*. You were right back where you started. So at the end of that, there's a bit of a hangover where people have to start again."

Like Sloan and Thrush Hermit, many east-coast bands were structured democratically, with everyone contributing to songwriting and decision-making. Colin Mackenzie calls this "a curse and a blessing." Having multiple songwriters, he says, created problems for each band as the members figured out which direction to go in. This was a recurring problem in the heady days of indie rock in the '80s and '90s, and it certainly wasn't restricted to the Maritimes. Jon Fine, the former member of Bitch Magnet and Coptic Light, chronicled the struggles of early American indie in the 2015 book *Your Band Sucks*, calling democratic bands "in practice, a huge pain, because anyone could veto anything, and did. Bands don't really work when they're communal endeavours. They require leaders." But Mackenzie also thinks this kind of structure helped pop explosion bands find their sound. "That's what made the scene the way it was — that sound of artists harmonizing, and multiple singer-songwriters, that kind of thing." Democracy is still a struggle for Sloan. "It's hard to keep a band together, let me tell you," says Chris Murphy. "Our band is only together because certain people are bending over backwards to keep other people happy." And when their bands ended, many musicians from that era stopped bending over backwards to keep the scene alive at home, too. "People are always leaving Halifax, but it felt like a lot of people were leaving around then," says Plumtree's Carla Gillis, who now lives in Toronto. "Everyone was kind of floating around figuring out what to do next."

But it put Halifax, and other east-coast cities like Moncton, on the map. Label interest may have plateaued after a while, Greg Clark says, but all the label and media interest helped his city in the long-term. Finally, he says, "being from Halifax was something people would be interested in checking out." To Peter Rowan, the scene they built up was proof that current, relevant music could be made in a region with a "narrow vision" that would rather celebrate cultural history than acknowledge its present successes.

Thrush Hermit had built up plenty of successes before they broke up. They were a full-time band for seven years and had two full-lengths, two EPs, and a stack of singles as trophies to show for it. "Their dream was to make a living and not bend, and they were real artists in that respect," Clyde Lieberman says. "At the point where they would have had to change, they decided not to change. They'd rather go up in a ball of flames than become something they didn't want to be." Plaskett wouldn't trade the Thrush Hermit experience for anything. "From the age of 13, we were playing music together, until the age of 25. And we had record deals, and there was exciting stuff going on. We went to California, New York, had all these experiences — nobody had been to these places, and we went and did all this together for the first time. It felt like we were in the Who."

The Hermit played their final show on December 11, 1999, at Halifax's Marquee Club. With his shaggy hair and clipped bangs, Plaskett channelled the image of a young Rod Stewart as the band burned through their set list. If an imbalanced democracy brought the band to its end, it wasn't entirely visible as the vest-clad Plaskett and Benvie, in a red leather jacket, traded lick after lick on their Gibsons through songs like "Oh My Soul" and "(Oh Man) What to Do." In a tribute to Mike Campbell — who filmed the proceedings — the band played his favourite song, "From the

Back of the Film," twice, since he'd always complained that the two-minute tune was too short. The ruthlessly shaggy Benn Ross kept time in the back, and McGettigan, in a sleeveless turtleneck, was just as excitable as ever as he sang on "Oh Man." And even though he'd long been sequestered to stage right, Benvie used the song to come to the front of the stage, past the monitors, to shred that song's final notes. But that was it. After seven years of bad luck and bad timing, Thrush Hermit came to an end in the final days of the 20th century.

The members went their separate ways. Benvie soon published his first book, *Safety of War*, and relocated to Montreal, where he shared an apartment with Peter Elkas, went to university, and joined the Dears. McGettigan kicked around Halifax for a while, recording bands and working on film shoots, eventually getting lured away to Toronto. As for Plaskett, he couldn't think of a more fitting time than the end of the millennium to close a chapter in his life — and to open a new one. Music was all he knew, and he still had some to make. So that New Year's Eve, he got into his Parisienne, drove to Cape Breton, and started building himself a new band.

WORK OUT FINE

IN THE EARLY '90s, a ragtag team of Halifax musicians started up a makeshift downtown street-hockey league in the parking lot of the Hollis Street liquor store. Among them was Matt Murphy, who played in the Super Friendz; Doug MacDonald, of No Damn Fears; and Dave Marsh, a disciple of the city's '80s punk scene, who would over time play for both of those bands. Marsh can remember one day, around 1993, when someone — probably Chris Murphy — pulled up in a K-car and a tall, scrawny, baby-faced kid climbed out of the passenger seat with a hockey stick.

All parties involved recall that the teenaged Joel Plaskett was not particularly great at the game. Marsh says it was like watching "some kind of Japanese pantomime." Plaskett insists that, for the most part, he enjoyed it. "They were all competitive older pricks," he says with a big grin. "I'm joking a little, though it got kind of aggressive for my liking. But it was fun."

As awkward as the game was, getting to know Marsh made Plaskett's post-Hermit life much easier. He had seen Marsh play before with No Damn Fears, but they didn't meet until Thrush Hermit had enough clout to start socializing with other bands. Sometime after that hockey game, Chris Murphy brought 18-year-old Plaskett over to Marsh's apartment to watch *Bad Lieutenant*. Both older musicians remember how funny it was that Plaskett was so young — seven years younger than Murphy, a dozen years younger than Marsh — as they watched Harvey Keitel jerk off and smoke crack.

A few years later, in 1997, future Sadies drummer Mike Belitsky came up from New York to play the Pop Explosion festival with his new band, Cheticamp, that'd just recorded with Tommy Ramone. He called Plaskett up to play pedal steel for the show and got Ian McGettigan on bass. Drumming along was Marsh, who'd played on the record. "I remember being totally blown away by his drumming," Plaskett says. Marsh was experienced and commanding, but he meshed quickly with the young musician. They jammed occasionally, at one point recording a handful of cover songs, with Chris Murphy in a tiny studio in the Khyber building. And when Plaskett started looking for a backing band to play shows behind *In Need of Medical Attention*, Marsh was one of his first calls.

They developed a push-pull friendship: when Plaskett's five-piece band went to New York in 1999 to play *Medical Attention* material at the CMJ music festival, Marsh taunted Plaskett by drinking beers in the Parisienne's backseat as he nervously drove through Manhattan. But on the way home, as Plaskett drove the sleeping band through a storm, Marsh kept the frontman awake, trading jokes with him about lonesome ghost truckers.

The five-piece called themselves the Joel Plaskett Emergency Band. Plaskett remembers naming it for the *Medical Attention* material, but Marsh thinks he might have had a hand in it. When Plaskett first realized he needed a backing band for the new songs, he approached Marsh and Andrew Glencross, possibly at another liquor-store hockey game. "I've got this solo album, and I've gotta put a band together," Marsh remembers Plaskett saying. "It's a bit of an emergency." One of the pair stopped him: "There's your band name."

HAVING SPENT NEARLY a decade in a democratic band, Plaskett wanted more control over his new material. The leaner the unit, the more control he'd have. He knew Marsh could help him flush out a fuller sound with fewer people onstage. A multi-instrumentalist, Marsh was actually on the cusp of returning to songwriting, and to the guitar, when Plaskett asked him to be his permanent drummer. He was nonetheless happy to oblige. "When you come up against somebody that progressive and capable, as a musician, you don't walk away from that," says Marsh. "You embrace that. Joel and I, we hooked on this very basic rock connection."

Marsh suggested that Tim Brennan, who he'd played with years before in Black Pool, should play bass. He insisted Brennan was the right fit: "Not only did he look like Paul Simonon from the Clash — he could actually *play* like Paul

The original Emergency power trio: Tim Brennan, Joel Plaskett, and Dave Marsh. [© Emily Falencki]

Simonon from the Clash." Brennan had just finished an MFA at York University in Toronto, and there were whispers he was moving back to town. Plaskett followed that tip to Brennan's family home in Cape Breton that New Year's Eve, and the bassist agreed to take part. Just a few weeks after Thrush Hermit called it quits, the Joel Plaskett Emergency power trio got to work.

Transitioning out of Thrush Hermit was jarring, but Plaskett didn't give himself much time to think about it. "It was a weird time, but it was also kind of seamless," he says. He, Marsh, and Brennan quickly started rehearsing at a space they renovated in the Khyber building. Plaskett had already written a handful of songs for what would have been Thrush Hermit's next LP, including "True Patriot

Love," "Clueless Wonder," "Waiting to Be Discovered," and "This Is a Message." The Hermit had even jammed on the riff from what would become "Down at the Khyber." But the Emergency was Plaskett's chance to play within a new power dynamic. "When that band got cookin', it was exciting," he says. "And all of a sudden I could write however I wanted."

AFTER YEARS OF living off record-industry advances — and buyouts — Plaskett took his first straight job at Nova Scotia's provincial archives in 2000, transferring old Canadian Broadcasting Corporation tapes onto CD. It was a mix of strange busywork and free time. He'd sometimes have to bake tapes in a fruit dehydrator so they wouldn't deteriorate in the dubbing process, but he had plenty of time to work on his website. He also had time to track down an email address for soul superstar Irma Thomas, whom he adored. He wrote her a note asking who drummed on her song "Wish Someone Would Care" and offered to send her some music: a cover of her song "The Hurt's All Gone" and an original she inspired called "Unconditional Love." She responded a half hour later with a P.O. box to send them to.* He still beams when he tells the story.

The archive gig was a nepotistic affair: Plaskett got the job after it was first offered to his mother, and once he started, he convinced the archive to hire his five-piece Emergency

---

* The mystery drummer was legendary session musician Earl Palmer, who'd also recorded with Sam Cooke, Ritchie Valens, and Neil Young.

bandmate Charles Austin to help him out. Because it was contract work, the pair was able to take time off to tour and record. This included making a debut full-length for Neuseiland, on which Austin played guitar and Plaskett drummed. And after months of dubbing tapes, rehearsing, and playing with the Emergency, Plaskett had enough practice and cash in hand to make a record of his own.

The band had been renting their Khyber jam space from Austin, who'd set up a studio on the building's third floor. It was officially named Ultramagnetic Recording, but everyone called it the Mullet, and it was natural place for Austin's friends to record. The Emergency set up camp at the studio in October 2000, with Austin as technical assistant and Plaskett as producer. Free of expectations, Plaskett set out to carve his own sound. To achieve that, he brought in a couple trusty weapons from his arsenal: his own TASCAM machine for that warm tape sound, and Ian McGettigan, who'd been Thrush Hermit's chief studio sound-sculptor. They recorded for a month, working 12 hours a day, rarely taking days off.

If *Clayton Park* is the sound of suburban kids embracing their classic-rock roots, *Down at the Khyber* is the soundtrack to Plaskett's move downtown — to the Khyber itself — making a scene and a sound of his own. Obsessed with Irma Thomas, he wanted to make his own *Down at Muscle Shoals*; the Stones might not have recorded at the Khyber, but for him, it's just as important a place. From the opening riff, it's clear that the ghost of Thrush Hermit still lingers, but there's a new endgame to this record, which channels both country and soul through the Khyber's century-old walls.

The title track might be a meditation on how touring toyed with his health, but it's a proclamation, too. He's been to North Dakota, the Rocky Mountains, and the potato state, but here — Halifax, the Khyber — is where he's making things happen.

When Plaskett first started travelling with Thrush Hermit, he says, "the geography of touring made it into the songs." He was simply writing about the life he knew — "which was away a lot." By the time he moved in with girlfriend Rebecca Kraatz in 1998, he was staying home a lot more. "In that transitional time, I started to think more about home, because I missed it more when I was away. I was getting older, and there was someone there that I wanted to return to." Other bits of biography appear throughout the record, including pop-explosion burnout in the reflective "Waiting to Be Discovered," and jabs at American cultural dominance couched in the love-is-lost "True Patriot Love."

Free from pressures of the democratic Hermit, Plaskett's musical influences on *Khyber* are all over the map: he covers Alton and Hortense Ellis's "Cry Together" with an alt-country bent, while channelling Irma Thomas's "Yours until Tomorrow" on "Unconditional Love." His guitar playing changed, too, as he learned to navigate both rhythm and lead parts in Rob Benvie's absence. *Khyber* was a necessary statement for Plaskett: an announcement that he was still alive, still kicking, still driven to play. "He was totally hungry," Austin says. "He really had something to prove, and made something awesome."

Plaskett and Rebecca Kraatz. [© Marrianne Kraatz]

WITHOUT A LABEL or manager, Plaskett became a shrewd businessman, handling everything himself. For local shows, he'd make his own black-and-white posters and "poster the shit out of the city myself." Staple gun in hand, he'd blanket Dalhousie University, then line Spring Garden Road and Gottingen Street — twice, usually, for each show, since people would tear them down. As the new band bounced back and forth between the Attic and the Marquee, audiences started filling out. They did a couple month-long residencies at Down in Hell, in the Marquee's basement, and fans would pack in, even on blustery January Mondays. "This was the first time we were drawing a crowd because of who we were," Plaskett says. "It was starting to cook."

"Once the three-piece hit, it was full steam ahead," Marsh says. "All we really wanted to do was play." It wasn't all easy; there was one show in Fredericton where only two people showed up, including Brennan's brother, and staff left the house music on as the band played. But Marsh says they were ready for sacrifices: "Be prepared to drive all night, pee in a bottle, and get paid $50. Yep, let's go."

In a sense, Plaskett was starting a career from scratch — but he'd also spent the Hermit years carefully building relationships with people who were now willing to help him out. "He knew he was going to be playing at a club four years from now, so he might as well treat someone well," McGettigan says. At one of the Hermit's last Toronto shows, a young booking agent named Tom Kemp handed Plaskett his card in case he ever came back to Ontario on a solo tour. When Plaskett called him up to make good on the offer, the agent was thrilled to help. Plaskett started looking for touring vehicles; with McGettigan's aid, he found an old Hydro-Québec truck — a '95 Chevy Suburban — in Oshawa, Ontario, that fit the bill. Armed with wheels and a booking agent, Plaskett and the Emergency began playing small shows around Ontario and started to build an audience away from home. Slowly, Thrush Hermit nostalgia gave way to a growing, genuine Emergency fanbase. "It was a lot of work on his part," Kemp says. "He was really grinding it out on the road. But each show was a little victory."

Longtime radio DJ Dave Bookman was one of the first people in Toronto to get his hands on a copy of *Khyber* in 2001. He'd long been a fan of Plaskett. "Right from the start, you knew there was something special about this big, tall gangly kid who had rock 'n' roll in his soul," Bookman says. He shared the new record with everyone he knew and was the first DJ to play Plaskett in the city, on 102.1 The Edge. "Not wanting him to be forgotten was a really important thing for me," Bookman says. "I began a decade-long crusade of getting Joel into the mainstream." He got *Khyber* in the hands of promoters Jeff Cohen and Craig Laskey, who booked the Horseshoe Tavern and Lee's Palace, and they joined the quest to make Toronto, home to Canada's music industry, fall in love with Joel Plaskett. "It's like the first Elvis Costello record — it was just totally different to us," Cohen says. With his new alt-country flavour, "we were actually more aligned musically with what Joel was doing solo than what he was doing with Thrush Hermit," says Cohen. "We became boosters, whatever that means. We got excited by it. We were like, 'Can we do more shows for you? Can we get you in to do more interviews?'"

The band's live show quickly fell into a groove, too. "There was a lot of band chemistry," Brennan says. Marsh calls it "semi-supernatural. It was just tight enough to be professional, and it was just un-tight enough to be garage-y as fuck."

The Emergency released *Khyber* in July 2001 through Halifax's Brobdingnagian Records. It got mild acclaim in Canada, including a 2002 Juno nomination for Alternative Album of the Year. Music journalist Bob Mersereau listed *Down at the Khyber* as No. 46 in his oft-cited list of Top 100 Canadian Albums, ahead of records by Neil Young, Shania Twain, and Gordon Lightfoot — as well as *Clayton Park*, which was No. 85. Hearing the record, critic Carl Wilson said Plaskett "stands out among the punk-bred musicians who have grown into an obsession with the craft of the rock

song. Big Star, Beach Boys, Beatles, Dylan, Neil Young —
you'll hear their traces less in radio hits than in the putative
underground." Meanwhile, former murderecords employee
Marc Brown, who'd bonded with Plaskett over Bruce
Springsteen, had moved to England and offered to release
Khyber there on his own label, Multiball. Brown released a
U.K.-exclusive *Clueless Wonder* seven-inch and managed to
get the record several reviews in the British press — including in *Q* magazine, which called it a "need-to-know guitar-
rock triumph" — garnering Plaskett enough attention to
play a handful of shows overseas. Some of them were even
solo, which Brown remembers Plaskett being nervous about
— "which, if you think back, is ridiculous."

BY THE TIME the album was released, Plaskett was making
enough money through music to get by and finished working at the archives. Ever frugal, he continued to handle all
of his affairs alone — including sitting on the floor every
three months to sort piles of receipts and fill out endless
tax forms. It meant he didn't have to answer to anyone or
compromise his work or lifestyle. He started to build a reputation as a troubadour, always hustling, always on the road,
always demoing.* And the question so many people asked
— when are you heading down the road to a bigger music
hub? — was soon turned on its head.

"I just never needed to leave," he says. "When I started

---

* One song from that era was "Cold Blue Light," which featured an unlikely
collaborator — Plaskett's sister, Anna, on French horn.

touring the country and out to Calgary, and all of a sudden there are all these Maritimers. Somebody holds up a Nova Scotia flag and is like, 'You stayed!' People are celebrating the fact that I'm from there, and I've come out from Nova Scotia. That 'Maritimers away' feeling became a celebration in other cities. So what initially might have been to my detriment suddenly began to work to my advantage. I didn't have to leave. Because if I left, people might be like, 'You left! You're not as interesting anymore!'"

Mike Campbell certainly thought he was interesting. Dave Marsh brought a pre-mastered copy of *Khyber* to the *MuchEast* host's house before it was released, and he was floored. "The longer the record went on, the better it got," Campbell says. "Like, *holy shit*, this is an astonishingly good record." On his show, he started playing *Khyber*'s videos — including "True Patriot Love," "Clueless Wonder," and "Maybe We Should Just Go Home" — as often as he could. He coaxed local rock station Q104 to do the same. Campbell, who was winding down his time at MuchMusic, saw big things for Plaskett, but believed he needed a manager to do it. He was sure the self-described control freak was, in fact, in control enough to handle his own affairs; there just weren't enough hours in the day to handle them completely on his own. Campbell thought his friend Sheri Jones, the manager who put a rock band behind fiddler Ashley MacIsaac in 1994 and propelled him to fame, would be a good fit.

Working with MacIsaac, though, had kept Jones so busy that she didn't know much about the Hermit or Plaskett. Campbell pestered her to listen to *Khyber* for weeks, but it wasn't until she bummed a ride home from downtown

Halifax on a frigid, taxi-less winter night that he got his way. "He got in the car and said, 'This is the price of the drive' — and he locked the doors and put on *Down at the Khyber*," Jones says. "And we went back to his place and played it two, three times. I was completely in love with the record."

The pair decided the best approach was if they both offered to co-manage Plaskett. They came to him with a simple pitch: he was ready for a record deal, but no one would sign him without dedicated management. He was initially hesitant, both because he was stubborn about handling his own affairs and because he didn't really know Jones. It took a few meetings and phone calls, but by late 2002, Plaskett decided she and Campbell would be a good fit. The managers developed a working dynamic: bed-by-10 Jones handled the day-to-day while night owl Campbell became Plaskett's chief cheerleader, building up audiences and stoking their excitement for shows.

Early in 2003, Campbell set up an East Coast Music Awards showcase at the Marquee Club with an all-star local lineup: the Trews, Matt Mays & El Torpedo, and the Joel Plaskett Emergency. Jones convinced a few industry executives to come, including Kim Cooke, the newly minted general manager of MapleMusic Recordings, which itself was a brand new imprint with Universal Music Group.

Cooke was familiar with Plaskett. He'd first met the musician at the ECMAs in 1993. "I can remember, very clearly, this tall, gangly teenager rushing up to me and thrusting a cassette in my hands," Cooke says. The tape was Thrush Hermit's *John Boomer*. At the time, Cooke was a month into being Warner Canada's head of A&R and listened to everything he got his hands on. He thought the tape was good, but not major-label material.

Then, he says, "I did a very smart thing." He wrote Plaskett a rejection letter: "To sum it up quickly, it's early days. Keep playing and writing, sharpening and refining and remember that no matter the genre of music, great songs are everything. I hope you'll keep me posted on your next move."

Almost exactly a decade later, Jones let Cooke know about that next move, inviting him to the big Saturday show at the Marquee and to a smaller gig that Friday at the World Trade & Convention Centre. It turned out Cooke was right in 1993 — genre really didn't matter. Plaskett didn't need to replicate his decade-old pop-rock sensibilities to write great songs. At the Friday show, Cooke says, "my jaw hit the floor." He remembers eyeing a rival A&R rep across the room and realizing he had to sign the Emergency. There was a handshake deal by the end of the weekend, and he made a formal pitch to Jones and Campbell at the Juno Awards in Ottawa a few months later. It wasn't a huge contract — MapleMusic was effectively independent, despite being a wing of Universal — but the label was keen on Plaskett and could showcase him to a wider audience than he'd get alone.

WITH MAPLEMUSIC'S BACKING, the Emergency set about making their next album. To say *Khyber*'s budget was shoe-string would be a vast understatement — McGettigan wound up squatting in a heatless apartment during its late-fall recording — so a budget for its follow-up was welcomed with open arms. While the Mullet had its charms as a cozy attic space in a storied arts centre, the deal afforded the band a bigger studio — one where they didn't need to lug their gear up three flights of stairs. Plaskett gathered the original *Khyber* team at Sonic Temple Recording Studio on Hollis Street in May 2003. Austin helped man the boards, and McGettigan — who'd by then moved to Toronto and was making a name for himself in recording — came back to co-produce.

The slicker studio had its ups and downs. "It wasn't as homey as the first album," bassist Brennan says. Marsh missed the tones that the last record managed to pull from the history-soaked Khyber walls. Both he and Austin sensed a change in direction, too — that the songs were more deliberately aimed for radio. When you put out a song called "Radio Fly," Marsh says, "you end up chasing the wind when you should be rowing your own boat." He was also trying to convince Plaskett to let him co-write a song for the record. Plaskett instead let him include a song of his own: "Heart to Heart With Lionel."

Truthfully, Truthfully, which emerged from the Sonic Temple sessions, marks a further step away from Thrush Hermit's sound. The guitar's still at the front, but walls of crunchy chords take a backseat to the spacious, alt-country, sometimes bluesy style Plaskett had begun to master as he got comfortable handling both rhythm and lead parts. The approach lends the lyrics plenty of room to breathe in tracks like "Work Out Fine," the Hermit-era "Come On Teacher," and the Tone-Lōc channelling "Extraordinary," all of which remain live staples. Nestled in the middle of the album,

"The Red Light" and "Radio Fly" are radio-pop singles that never were. The record's back half turns to heartbreak, as the songs' characters face disaster, watch loved ones walk away, and search for things they've never seen. While Plaskett sings less explicitly about Nova Scotia on *Truthfully* than he did on *Khyber*, a reality of life there creeps into the songs instead: people have a tendency to ship away.

Plaskett's renown has long hinged on his live performances, which he often augments with vivid stories peppered between and within songs. But his storytelling habit extends to the songs themselves, too, and *Truthfully* makes for a good study of executing narratives without falling victim to tropes of old. There is a tradition in Maritime song to write about going away — about industry collapsing, of heading for the Prairies — that writers like Stan Rogers and Stompin' Tom Connors basked in. Plaskett has always found that approach a little dramatic. But at this time in his life, the east coast's outflow of people was getting personal, and it comes through lyrically, though with a lighter touch than his forebears. Many of *Truthfully*'s songs, some more explicitly than others, touch on the themes of leaving and loss. "Everybody's left this town," Plaskett sings in "All the Pretty Faces," as a chorus asks, "Who could blame them?" There's the Montreal-Toronto burn on "Work Out Fine." And on "The Day You Walked Away": "You blew the doors wide open, and everybody ran."

Here and elsewhere, Plaskett sees himself as a short-story author. He doesn't usually live his own lyrics, but instead finds relatable themes and sticks to them, injecting other perspectives into his own first-person narratives for the sake of a good yarn. In the tales of *Truthfully*, the exodus he sings about is real. McGettigan, Benvie, the guys from Sloan, and countless others who he'd spent the previous decade with had packed up and headed west. As afraid as he is of "woe-is-me" lyrics, Curtis Mayfield's approach to love and loss inspired him to write about it honestly. "It's funny," he says. "So many people from that era didn't come back to Halifax. When you're young, you think everyone's gonna be here, for some reason. You don't think about people leaving until you get to your mid-20s, and you're like, *Wait — okay, people are digging in their heels somewhere and they're not coming back.* They meet someone, their life changes, and they're gone."

Shortly after the album was recorded, Plaskett bought a house across the Halifax harbour in Dartmouth, reaffirming this allegiance to Nova Scotia to *Exclaim!* magazine as he re-shingled his roof post–Hurricane Juan: "I take a certain amount of pride living out here, and my way of giving back to it is to write about what it's like to be here." Of course, not everyone left, and it wasn't the end of the world — but Plaskett sticks to his themes, even if that means embellishing. "Whatever perspective you're taking, you should hardline it for the sake of the song. There's nothing worse than a really wishy-washy perspective on a tune." This approach is not exclusive to his more serious material. In "Extraordinary," for instance, he sings about burning leaves in his own backyard, when, in reality, he'd watched his neighbour's son make a leaf fire so big the fire department showed up. "I thought, *It's better if I put in the first person*," he says, "because then it's badass."

THE EMERGENCY RELEASED *Truthfully, Truthfully* in October 2003, and Canadian media started to heap on what would eventually be a career's worth of near-unilateral praise. This may be because Canadians are too polite to shun the most nationalist of the artists they profile, writing either positively or not at all; or it could be, in part, that many journalists can relate to the early career setbacks of Thrush Hermit. "If F. Scott Fitzgerald famously claimed that there are no second acts in American lives," the *Globe and Mail*'s Carl Wilson wrote about the album, "it may be just as useful a fiction to propose that in Canadian lives, there are no first acts." The *Montreal Gazette* framed the record as the start of something big for the Emergency: "They have the sentimental side down pat, and a few more moments when the needle jumps into the red could send them through the roof." Critical acclaim and legitimate label support helped them embark on bigger tour dates, but Plaskett & Co. were already establishing themselves as relentless road warriors and had grown much of their audience on their own. "You go and you do it, and the audience builds and the word spreads," he says. "I've always built it on word of mouth — *Oh, have you seen this dude?*" They packed Lee's Palace in Toronto, and in Edmonton and Calgary, home to legions of both Thrush Hermit fans and displaced Maritimers, they'd play to 500 or 600 people a night. The Emergency spent part of the next year touring the country with the Tragically Hip, including, on Canada Day 2004, playing the Molson Amphitheatre in Toronto — this time void of Steve Miller Band covers.

Even as the shows got bigger, Plaskett would sign autographs and talk to every last fan before he'd pack up the

As the Emergency grew their Canadian audience, they still played plenty at home — including at the Khyber, where it all began. [© Greg Baller]

Suburban. These fans were the reason Plaskett could put a roof over his head, and he always made sure he returned their attention. The spotlight around him was growing, but not big enough to shine on everybody he had onstage.

AROUND THE TIME *Truthfully* was released, Tim Brennan stopped playing every Emergency show. His wife, Emily Falencki, had moved to Ireland for grad school, and he moved over with her, usually only coming back for major tours. Ian McGettigan began filling in — but within a year, he was doing it more and more regularly.

"It was around that time that I bowed out of it," Brennan says. He knew Plaskett thought the world of him, but being in the band made the rest of his life a struggle. Even when he was living in Nova Scotia, the obligation of the Emergency made his day job — teaching photography at NSCAD — difficult. He and his wife wanted to have kids, too. So when he weighed where the band was going against the rest of his life, he felt he didn't have much of a choice. "It was starting to become less of a three-piece rock 'n' roll band, and I could see Joel had other intentions, doing lots of acoustic numbers in the set. That was great for the audience, but as a bass player, it was a little less of an interesting gig for me. I knew from the first time I saw him that this was what he was gonna do for the rest of his life. I wasn't going to put the rest of my life on hold for his career."

He explained his reasons to Plaskett and Marsh. The split was amicable, though it frustrated Marsh, who loved how the trio had meshed onstage. But, he says, "when Old Brennan makes up his mind, that door has shut." Luckily, Marsh was a big fan of Brennan's replacement — and, as he puts it, the replacement's "eloquent anarchy."

That anarchy was peddled by McGettigan, who soon injected his antics into the band's touring adventures on a full-time basis. When *Truthfully* was nominated for the Alternative Album of the Year Juno in 2004, he was already playing with the band regularly, and came in tow. On the way home, he tried to board the aircraft using only an expired library card as ID. Naturally, he didn't make the plane. Later, at another airport, as he passed through security in an 1890s-style boater hat and tank top, the metal detector beeped at his crotch. He was forced to reveal that he'd been fastening his pants together with a half-dozen safety pins.

"McGetts brought the same earthiness that Timmy always had," Marsh says, "but with that extra special bit of Salvador Dalí touch." The bassist Plaskett bet everything on when the Hermit called it quits was gone, but a former Hermit had stepped up for the job. The Emergency remained intact, and he was still among friends. Some — but not all — of them would soon join him on his next adventure.

HAPPEN NOW

BY 2003, CHRIS MURPHY and the rest of Sloan had been living in Toronto for more than half a decade. It'd been years since Joel Plaskett had been able to regularly hang out with Murphy, his old friend, neighbour, and early career champion. Plaskett was visiting California early that year, and, as it happened, Sloan was there, too, recording with Tom Rothrock. So he and Murphy got together and took a drive out to Joshua Tree National Park, showing each other demos that would eventually turn into *Action Pact* and *Truthfully, Truthfully*. One of the unfinished songs Murphy played had a catchy, repetitive chorus: "I love this town," over and over again. It was Plaskett's favourite, Murphy says, and the one he kept asking to hear.

When Plaskett released his second solo album, *La De Da*, in 2005, it was anchored, in part, by an ode to Halifax called "Love This Town." Plaskett hardly remembers Murphy's song of the same name. "You don't really know, when you're writing songs, where you're channelling stuff from," he says. "I'm not saying I stole the song. I didn't. I wrote it. I think of that song as a shameless Al Tuck ripoff, to be honest."

Plaskett doesn't hide the influence Tuck and Murphy have had on his songwriting. "The mark of the Halifax writing and music scene that I've always loved and wanted to be a part of — and I think I've carried on that tradition — is this mix of humour and melancholy and pointedness." The tradition, he says, recognizes the unique attitude of Halifax, and all of the Maritimes, including the region's inherent outsider perspective, like Tuck did on songs like the pop-explosion takedown "One Day the Warner." "There's certain traits that I saw in writers, like Al, from P.E.I., who can mix humour and sadness. Chris had that with 'I Am the Cancer.' I'm not saying every song did it, but there was a general vein through the music that I really like. You write for your peers, you write for your town, and you take it seriously, but you don't take it *so* seriously."

Murphy was never happy with his original track, and it never made the cut for *Action Pact*. Only years later did it emerge, heavily rewritten, as "All I Am Is All You're Not," on 2008's *Parallel Play*. But the ever-sarcastic musician relished the unintended intellectual property theft, using it as an excuse to throw shade at his old scenemate. "Whenever I saw him next," he says, "I was like, 'Hey, I like your song. And I liked it even better when it was my song.'" Murphy's jabs, though, are in jest. He does love Plaskett's song. "His story's way better. I had a dilemma about what town to be writing about: Halifax or Toronto? I love *what* about

Chris Murphy and Plaskett at Joshua Tree National Park.
[From Joel Plaskett's archives]

Toronto — the mayor?* I feel like I'm just barging in on history, because I feel like that song will go down as one of the great songs. And I had a small part in it."

"Love This Town" is a song perfectly befitting Plaskett's career, with a backstory perfectly befitting the song. It's a collection of stories and homages from home and abroad — from Tuck's apartment burning down, to a hat-tip to Springsteen's "Bobby Jean," to the long drive home from Ontario — all wrapped into a love letter to Halifax. With its balanced blend of fun and sorrow, it's a road-show anchor and a hometown anthem. The song even takes a dig at the musicians Plaskett has watched leave Nova Scotia, which, ironically, includes Sloan. Halifax *Chronicle-Herald* music reporter Stephen Cooke says, "It validates his decision to stay in such a beautiful way." The song resonates with people

---

* Rob Ford was Toronto's mayor at the time of this interview.

of all stripes: in 2015, longtime federal cabinet minister Peter MacKay, a Nova Scotian, quoted it when he announced he was leaving politics. Not only does "Love This Town" exemplify everything that's helped Plaskett build a successful career without having to leave home, it spreads that home's gospel from coast to coast to coast. "People celebrate it," he once said. "They have their own experiences that they relate it to. It takes on a life of its own."

When he recorded the biggest hometown tribute of his career, he was about as far away from home as his truck could take him.

A LITTLE WHILE after *Khyber* was released, Plaskett got an email from a fan in Arizona named Bob Hoag. Hoag had been a Thrush Hermit fan since a Canadian boarding-school roommate introduced him to their music a decade earlier. He'd kept up with Plaskett's career, fell in love with *Khyber*, and even drove to Los Angeles to see one of the first U.S. Emergency shows. He'd just set up his own recording studio, Flying Blanket, and wanted to take a month off. And if he wasn't getting paid anyway, he thought, why not make a record for someone he likes?

After he saw pictures of Charles Austin's recording space on a message board, he thought he might have nicer gear than the Mullet could provide — and sent Plaskett, out of the blue, an offer to make his next record. Plaskett remembers his first reaction: "Whoa, weird." But he looked Hoag up online and eventually got on the phone with him to talk it over. Plaskett explained he couldn't get a Canadian grant for a record if he made it at an American studio, and politely declined. He went and made *Truthfully* in Halifax, but once that album cycle slowed down, Plaskett started thinking about taking an adventure. He emailed Hoag again: sure, he'd take up that offer.

In May 2004, Plaskett packed up his Chevy Suburban, said goodbye to Kraatz, and headed for Arizona. He played a show in Philadelphia, stopped in Memphis to record some demos with his old pal Doug Easley, saw J.J. Cale play in Austin. Along the drive, he began humming a melody and hashing out some verses for a track he'd call "Love This Town." He drove through "biblical" hail and through Tornado Alley in Texas, gathering enough inspiration to finish a song he'd started the previous year, after Hurricane Juan devastated much of the Maritimes. He called it "Natural Disaster." By June 5, the day Ronald Reagan died, he'd made it to West Texas and stopped in the barely there town of Fort Stockton when the threat of tornadoes got too real. Stuck in a motel, he wrote a song about a woman he heard through the wall pleading to her lover, named Albert, that she wasn't cheating on him. A few days later he arrived at Hoag's home in Mesa, Arizona, outside of Phoenix, in time for an afternoon barbecue, sunburned blood-red on his left side from driving with the window down.

Hoag had gotten nervous while he waited for that moment. "Joel was my favourite singer-songwriter, and sometimes it's better not to get to know your heroes in person. They could end up being jerks." But, Hoag says, "this was the opposite of that."

Since Plaskett didn't know Hoag well, he asked Ian

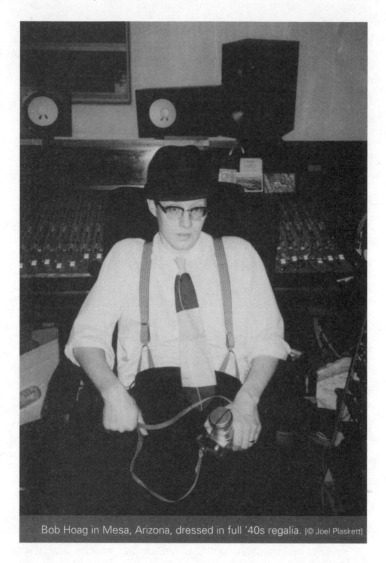

Bob Hoag in Mesa, Arizona, dressed in full '40s regalia. [© Joel Plaskett]

McGettigan to come along as a safety net. But Plaskett arrived a few days before his old Hermit pal flew in from Toronto, and he needed to kill some time. He and Hoag started doing some pre-production and test recordings, sometimes with just a single ribbon mic between the singer and his acoustic guitar in the booth. There was a rushed element to the sessions, as the lifelong Nova Scotian struggled to play in the Arizona heat. The studio's control room was air conditioned, but not the booth itself. "I was doing things as fast as humanly possible, 'cause I was sweating my ass off," Plaskett says. But in their rush, some gems surfaced: the final versions of both "Absentminded Melody" and "Love This Town" emerged from those early acoustic sessions.

McGettigan arrived later in the week, and the crew got to work on the meat of the album. To stave off the heat, they would wait until 5 or 6 p.m. to go to the studio and worked well through the night. Even then, the Canadians sweated it out in tank tops and undershirts. Meanwhile, the well-acclimated Hoag, a fanatic of '40s style, wore vintage wool suits every day as though it were nothing.

Earlier in 2004, at a Halifax music store, Plaskett found a tenor guitar — a bright-sounding four-stringed guitar curiously absent from much of pop music — and started to fool around with it. He called up his dad and told him he should check it out. Bill Plaskett came down, fell in love with the instrument, and bought it. The younger Plaskett immediately borrowed it. At home, he tuned it to open C and noodled around until he found a riff he liked. In Mesa, that riff turned into "Happen Now." He'd buy his own tenor guitar in Kingston, Ontario, on the way home from Arizona, and it became his writing tool for many other songs — among them "Soundtrack for the Night," "Beyond, Beyond, Beyond," and "I'm Yours." He now owns five of them.

Hoag, Plaskett, and McGettigan worked on the record through most of June. As the sessions wound down, Hoag

tried to convince Plaskett to play a show in Mesa. He obliged
— and, to Hoag's delight, invited the producer to play drums.
They rehearsed a mix of Plaskett's old and new material.
After practising the Hermit's "From the Back of the Film,"
Hoag immediately transitioned into the drumbeat from
McGettigan's "(Oh Man) What to Do," startling the bassist.
"*Clayton Park* is one of my all-time favourite records," Hoag
says. "I knew how to play every drum part." At the end of the
sessions, the trio rented out a local women's centre for a one-
time-only performance of both Plaskett and Hermit songs,
including "Oh Man." "It was probably one of the most special
things I ever really got to be part of," Hoag says.

McGettigan flew home, and Plaskett drove the Suburban
up the west coast, picking up Kraatz in British Columbia
for half the drive back to Nova Scotia, then ex–Local Rabbit
Peter Elkas for the other half, playing shows along the way.
Plaskett flew back to Mesa later that summer to mix the
record, which he named *La De Da*. He and Hoag became
good friends; Hoag and his wife, Kate, named Plaskett and
Kraatz the godparents of their first son. Plaskett regularly
tells the story in concert: he followed his gut and drove to
Arizona, and came back with a free record and a godson.

ABSENT FROM THE Arizona sessions was Dave Marsh, who
spent the early summer wondering why the Emergency
wasn't playing any shows. He found out the reason entirely
by mistake. As he loaded his drums into a cab, the driver
asked if he played in a band. Yes, Marsh responded, the Joel
Plaskett Emergency. "Oh yeah," the driver said. "I heard Joel

went down to Texas to record an album." Not quite Arizona, but close — and enough of a surprise to make Marsh fume. "Not only did I not know they were recording an album, but I had a taxi driver tell me."

He says he likes the songs that came out of the sessions — "I like songs off everything Joel does" — but still hasn't fully broached the subject with Plaskett. "I'm still a little bit in the dark. I don't research these things. It would have been nice to be informed that you're not working for the next year — that's all."

Marsh is known for being very direct, if not a dash abrasive, though many people who know him consider that to be a charm when it comes to his friendship with Plaskett, keeping the younger musician on his toes in the studio and onstage. The story of the Emergency is, in a sense, the story of Plaskett and Marsh's friendship and musical bond. But *La De Da* created a tension between the two that they've never fully resolved, in spite of their brotherly connection.

In part, that's because the direction that Brennan predicted for Plaskett began to come true. For *La De Da*, Plaskett wanted to make a record on his own terms, much like he wanted to shape his post-Hermit career: unbridled by excess baggage, free to do things at his own speed, with room to improvise. With no expectations for *La De Da* — he didn't tell his label about the trip, either — Plaskett was free to try something new. He wanted to make songs up on the fly, which is difficult with the costs and expectations that come with a band.

"'I'm not always at my most relaxed when I'm around the people that I know the best," Plaskett says. "I mean, I brought

Ian down because him and I go way, way back, and there's a lot we can do without having a discussion. But just being in that unknown land of Bob Hoag's universe made it good for me. I need the variety. I can't do the same thing with the same people all the time. I've always been true to the band — it's not like I pick up session bands all the time. But the desire to want to go and do things on my own still exists."

Over time, Marsh has grown to understand and acclimatize to the varying projects in Plaskett's career. And he's cool with that, as long as they still get to play together. "I've been there since the beginning," Marsh says. "I've crossed the country 25 times. I've played the $25 gigs. I own the Emergency brand through shared effort. But Joel's the name, and that's fair dues, because Joel has worked his ass off to get there."

AT FIRST, PLASKETT wasn't entirely sure what to do with the songs from the Arizona sessions, toying with the idea of turning them into a record he'd only sell at shows. Eventually, he decided to give them an official release. The Emergency-free, downtempo, more acoustically driven *La De Da* surprised his business team. "It wasn't what I wanted to hear," says Mike Campbell, who was unashamedly a huge fan of the Emergency's rock sound. But he was swayed once he heard the record. Sheri Jones was an immediate fan and sent it along to MapleMusic with an ultimatum to release it. "We were initially confused by it," says Kim Cooke, then Maple's manager. "It was a matter of figuring out what to do with it, in terms of how to market and promote it."

Opening with "Absentminded Melody" and ending with "Love This Town," *La De Da* is roughly sequenced along a journey to Arizona and back again. Plaskett looks back on the Thrush Hermit days ("Absentminded"), daydreams at the provincial archives ("Lying on a Beach," "Television Set"), drives south ("Nina and Albert," "Natural Disaster"), and comes back armed with a love letter for home ("Love This Town"). "*La De Da* might have warranted a trip away, but all roads eventually point home for Joel Plaskett," Vish Khanna wrote in *Exclaim!* Any lingering label skepticism was quickly cast aside when the media got ahold of it: critics called it a "jaw-dropping" record among his best works, with a laid-back feel that "doesn't undercut its pop appeal." It became Plaskett's best-selling record since the end of Thrush Hermit, and stocked his acoustic catalogue enough that he was able to play full-length solo shows more regularly. The widening sonics of his repertoire drew attention to the growing number of parallels to Bruce Springsteen: Nova Scotia as New Jersey, Emergency as E Street, and Arizona as Nebraska, if much less bleak.

Plaskett followed the record's 2005 release with the Alone and Together cross-Canada tour with old friend Peter Elkas, who opened with a short set of material, then supported a headlining Plaskett. The pair flew to British Columbia before the tour and bought an '89 Camry, put their guitars in the trunk and their merch in the backseat, and joked that as they headed east and sold their wares, they'd gradually fill the backseat with cash. The gigs were smaller than Emergency shows, as they played cafes and small songwriting venues across the country. They played

Peter Elkas and Plaskett in the '89 Camry, with merch stashed in the backseat. [From Joel Plaskett's archives]

multiple nights in bigger cities — a pair at Vancouver's Media Club, another in Toronto's Hugh's Room — while paying heed to smaller towns that rarely see touring musicians, from Canmore, Alberta, to North Bay, Ontario.

The tour gave a boost to Plaskett's storyteller persona. Both the Emergency and Thrush Hermit had a habit of improvising live, but on this tour, suddenly onstage alone with just a guitar, he began to trade long jams for extended stories — now considered an essential part of Plaskett concerts. "That was a really good tour in terms of showing people I could put on a different kind of show," Plaskett says. "It really meant that I could hit as many nooks and crannies in Canada as would have me. That's been a really important aspect to my development as a performer — being able to tour solo or duo and get into places that the band wasn't gonna get to for booking or financial reasons. That was a huge part of building the audience in Canada."

ON CANADA DAY in 2001, the Emergency shared a bill with the blues-reggae band Big Sugar at a concert on Citadel Hill, a historic park at the centre of downtown Halifax. Plaskett and Big Sugar's frontman, Gordie Johnson, got to chatting about ZZ Top, and, at a later show at the Marquee, Johnson coaxed Plaskett onstage to join them for a cover of the bearded band's "Waitin' for the Bus." Johnson liked his playing, though Plaskett is positive no one could hear his guitar beneath Johnson's deafening trademark double-neck.

They became acquaintances just as Johnson was becoming a fan of the Maritimes. After producing the Trews' 2003 record *House of Ill Fame,* the Big Sugar frontman became a regular visitor. At the same time, MapleMusic was encouraging Plaskett to push the envelope for his next record. Many around him — including Mike Campbell and Dave Marsh — thought Johnson would be the right fit to produce something different. Something big. Plaskett, whose solo career had so far been almost entirely self-produced, was initially hesitant. But he was fascinated by Johnson's punchy, compression-heavy production style: everything in the foreground, with the broad strokes of a KISS record, sonic depth traded for hooky breadth. After getting to know Johnson, he agreed to give it a shot — though only, at first, for an EP.

The Big Sugar frontman had by then relocated from Canada to Texas, where he worked regularly at Willie

Nelson's Pedernales Studios near Austin. To gear up for the recording sessions, Plaskett had to play his song ideas to Johnson over the phone. One of the drafts he played opened with the line "Hey, good lookin'," and Plaskett told Johnson that he'd probably change the words, since he'd borrowed the line from Hank Williams. Johnson's reaction was immediate: "Hell no, you're not." He saw something special in Plaskett and didn't want self-doubt to hold him back.

In October 2005, the Emergency convened in Toronto, gathering for two days at Sloan's west-end rehearsal space to practise. The band then headed to Phase One Studios in Scarborough with Johnson and made the Emergency's poppiest, most polished recordings to date — complete with guest piano and organ by Ian McLagan, Rod Stewart's former bandmate in the Faces. "A Million Dollars" echoes with kettle drums, while "Make a Little Noise" bursts with synths and organ sounds. On "Nowhere with You," Marsh insisted on changing the standard-issue rock beat Plaskett had in mind. "It's just got such a wicked, Buddy Holly, old school, '50s, innocent lyric to it that I went into the beat from 'Peggy Sue,'" he says of the galloping drumbeat he added, giving the song a radio-pop urgency.

As the sessions wound to a close, Johnson called Trews guitarist John Angus MacDonald and told him to come by the studio, preferably with booze. He arrived with a bottle of rum and a crew in tow, including bandmate Jack Syperek and sister Kate MacDonald. As they celebrated the recordings' end, Kate recorded part of the call-and-response chorus of "A Million Dollars," and everyone on site stepped into the booth for the gang vocals on "Nowhere with You."

THE 2005 JOHNSON sessions would be the only Emergency recordings to feature McGettigan on bass. Over dinner earlier that year, he told Plaskett he wanted out. He'd been living in Toronto since 2001 and was getting regular production work there, which made playing in a Halifax band difficult. He'd also started a new band of his own — with Rob Benvie, who'd left Montreal and moved to Toronto. The pair had begun to play together again, making electronic-leaning music as Camouflage Nights, and it was taking up more and more of their time. "I wanted to focus on my own thing, and Joel needed to have somebody in the same city to be in his band," McGettigan says. "The timing was right for everything." He played his final show with the band on New Year's Eve 2005 at the Marquee.*

Left alone in the rhythm section once again, Marsh was frustrated. He tried to convince Plaskett to bring in someone he already liked, suggesting Paul Boudreau of Cool Blue Halo. "But lo and behold," Marsh says, "Plaskett goes out of his way yet again and surprises me with the Elk."

"The Elk" is Chris Pennell, who was then a 22-year-old bassist from Dartmouth, playing in the bands Slight Return and Yellow Jacket Avenger. He'd met Plaskett entirely by coincidence. The lanky songwriter had taken the Charlottetown band Two Hours Traffic under his wing in the mid-2000s, producing a handful of their early records.

---

* Camouflage Nights signed to a major label, got attention for a Stars remix they did with Kevin Drew, and prepared a debut album, only to fall into a "legal brouhaha" for years, according to Benvie. Following a familiar narrative, the record was finally released by Sonic Unyon in 2012. "The moral of our story," Benvie says, "is don't sign with major labels."

One night after recording them at Charles Austin's studio atop the Khyber, the group went down to the building's event space while Yellow Jacket Avenger was playing. Hearing that Pennell lived in Dartmouth, he bummed a ride home across the Halifax harbour.

Pennell was happy to oblige, and they got to chatting along the drive. "I don't know if I knew anybody was leaving the band, but I said, 'Hey, if you're ever looking for someone to play the bass, I'd totally be up for it.'" A few months later, in the summer of 2005, Plaskett followed up. He emailed Pennell, who'd just left university and was driving a taxi to support his music habit, mentioning that McGettigan might be leaving the Emergency — and asked if they could get together and learn a few songs. They jammed in Plaskett's basement and recorded some demos at the Mullet. Pennell was young, but experienced, committed, and eager to tour. To Marsh's chagrin, Plaskett invited Pennell to join the Emergency that fall when the band got back from recording in Toronto.

"I come to this rehearsal session, and here's this six-foot-three mountain of a bass player, all of 22 years old," Marsh says. "I didn't know whether to shake his hand or dropkick him." Much of his fear was of not being able to connect on pop-culture reference points — "I don't wanna play with some fuckin' young guy who doesn't know who the Small Faces are," Plaskett mockingly quotes Marsh — but the bassist and drummer quickly clicked. "We bumped heads in the early days," Marsh says. "He was a mama's boy who was not used to being told no. But, as it turned out, Chris and I became good friends. And once again that may come down to Joel Plaskett's farsightedness." They've since become a playful pair onstage: at a recent Toronto show, Pennell handed bass duties over to surprise guest McGettigan for the show-closing "Come On Teacher"; he ran behind Marsh's drumkit, played along, and, for the show's grand finale, let the drummer smash a cymbal off his head.

Before McGettigan left the band, Mike Campbell suggested the Emergency put out a DVD to showcase their live show as a way to shop the band around outside of Canada. He had a theory: "If you watch this, and you still don't get it, then you're never gonna get it. It'll save us a bunch of travel time and a bunch of bullshit." By then he had left MuchMusic, but he called some friends who were still involved with the station and filmed a packed Marquee show. It was one of his last moves as co-manager, as he soon turned his duties over to Jones in order to run the Carleton, a Halifax music bar.

With bonus footage from the Alone and Together tour and Plaskett's complete suite of music videos, the band released the DVD called *Make a Little Noise* through MapleMusic. It eventually went Gold in Canada, selling more than 5,000 copies. Both the DVD and subsequent versions of *La De Da* were packaged with the Johnson sessions EP, also called *Make a Little Noise* — a necessary move to give a mountain of new fans something to buy as they fell hard for "Nowhere with You."

Plaskett had never been a radio staple, but that was about to change. MapleMusic licensed "Nowhere with You" for a commercial promoting the now-defunct department store Zellers. Radio station managers took notice of the song and started giving it great rotation — higher than Plaskett had ever had before. "I don't know if it would have gotten added if it weren't for that Zellers ad, which is really funny," Plaskett says. In bars and online, hipsters started invigorated debates as to whether Plaskett had sold out by shilling for the chain, but for him, it was a simple career move. He was no longer preoccupied with the indie-cred fears that made Thrush Hermit pass on the *Dumb and Dumber* soundtrack. "If you turn down those opportunities, then it hurts all the people who work on your behalf — your manager, your band, your family. I'd think twice if it was some kind of giant cigarette campaign, but I'm not too precious about it." Marsh, as usual, is less reserved with his opinion: "'Nyah, you sold out to Zellers' — as if that isn't the funniest Canadian sentence of all time. My mom bought every pair of sneakers for me from primary to grade seven from Zellers. Zellers has done me well."

"Nowhere with You" turned into a gateway drug for new fans, exposing the Emergency to a much larger audience that was eager to sink its teeth into all the other material they had to offer. The band immediately started playing bigger venues across the country in 2006 — the Phoenix in Toronto, the Commodore Ballroom in Vancouver — and dipped down into the United States, too. Nearly a decade after its release, the song remains the Emergency's best seller on iTunes. And thanks to the DVD, the band even played Australia after catching the eye of local promoter Geoff Trio, who helped them release an exclusive Australian compilation of Plaskett's songs as a vehicle for "Nowhere with You."

The shows had a whole new feel for the band. "I've never

Dave Marsh and Chris Pennell at the Pavilion in Halifax, after a group of kids rushed the stage and caused it to collapse. [© Jon Hutt]

really been part of a song that was a semi-hit, so it's funny how people react," Marsh says. "It's not that they're reacting to the music so much as they're reacting to the fame. There really is something about the fame of a song that unites people; that's why people feel free to associate that song with a good time."

As the summer of 2006 wound down, Plaskett managed to set aside some personal time, marrying Rebecca Kraatz — by then his sweetheart of 12 years — in August. But after that, it was time to prepare material for a follow-up to *Make a Little Noise*. With a hit single under his belt, Plaskett's label and management assumed his next logical step would be to write another radio hit. He had other plans.

SOUNDTRACK FOR THE NIGHT

BEFORE HE PRODUCES a record for an artist, Gordie Johnson likes to spend a day with them, drinking red wine and espresso, listening to records, trading stories about the musicians they've played with. In late 2006, fresh on the heels of the *Make a Little Noise* EP and tasked with a full-length follow-up, Johnson went to Dartmouth for his ritual. "In the end, the record usually ends up sounding like everything that happens that first day — including the red wine and the coffee and the scratchy records," he says. He and Joel Plaskett listened to Bruce Springsteen, and Richard and Linda Thompson, and the wine started to kick in. After a while, they reached a "euphoric state," Johnson says, and realized most of the songs Plaskett had lined up were parts of the same story. Then one of them — Johnson can't remember which — uttered two words that changed the whole direction of the project: "rock opera."

It was, at first, a half-hearted joke. "We were laughing to the point of spitting wine through our noses," Johnson says. But Plaskett pulled out his laptop and started rearranging his song ideas. "Well, what if you put the songs in this order? *This* order?" he asked the producer. "Does the story make sense?"

It did. If *Twice Removed* is an allegory for Halifax's isolation from the rest of the world, then the record they conceived that day — *Ashtray Rock* — is about life removed a step further, about 20 minutes west of downtown. On the surface, it's literally a rock opera about a rock — one tucked in a clearing in the woods of Clayton Park, where teenagers go to escape the boredom of a suburb on the edge of an already far-flung city. But *Ashtray Rock* isn't about how that's a bad thing. It's about recognizing what shapes you and finding meaning in it, no matter what city or what clearing or what band you're in. The story isn't autobiography, but the pieces are: the band, the rock in the woods, the mystery girl from out west, the romance of sharing music. When those pieces came together, they formed Plaskett's most personal, most cohesive, and most relatable record to date.

AS HE WAS writing the songs that showed up on the *Make a Little Noise* EP, Plaskett found himself riffing on a theme. With "A Million Dollars," he'd channeled an us-against-the-world sentiment that showed up, to a similar extent, in "Make a Little Noise." "I was really into that romantic world of music and the feeling you could have with somebody else and your records," he says. He'd also demoed a song called "Soundtrack for the Night" that toyed with the same themes, but he wasn't satisfied with it by the time he got to Scarborough. As he got ready to follow up the EP, though, words — and a narrative — started to come together: "A story about dudes driving around in a car listening to music."

On paper, that premise is frighteningly banal, but it served as a crucial framing device for his own past. As much as the story of Thrush Hermit was defined on tour and in the studio, a huge chunk of the band's early course was charted on long, aimless drives around Halifax as they waited for something to happen. Formative experiences like that helped shape Plaskett and the friendships that filled his younger days.

Other elements of his personal history started rolling into the story, too. "We had a band. It broke up. And running parallel to that band was my relationship with my wife, Rebecca, who I wouldn't have met if I wasn't playing music. Even though a girl didn't split up the band — that isn't the case — I fictionalized a version of how we get older, and I put it into the framework of the last year of high school, 'cause everybody there knows their lives are gonna change." It's during these final high school days that you realize you can't have everything all the time, he says. "Once you start a relationship, your relationship with somebody else changes, especially if the relationships are intense enough. And all that is glued together by music, because so many of the great people in my life, I've met because of it."

Plaskett had a framework, but if he was going to go through with a full-fledged rock opera, he needed a setting.

Thrush Hermit in Clayton Park, with Rob Benvie in the foreground, and his mom's Ford Tempo back right. In the early days, the band would spend endless hours driving around the city in that car.
[© Bill Plaskett]

He'd already borrowed storylines from familiar places to beef up the story at hand. Here, too, he took a page from an old friend: Rob Benvie.

"When you're a teenager, you spend all your time walking around your neighbourhood," Benvie says. "You avoid adults, and maybe get into some tomfoolery." In the late '80s, a pair of his friends stumbled upon a small clearing in the woods near a reservoir in Clayton Park. They called it Ashtray, for the crevice between two rocks where they'd throw their cigarette butts. Over time, the lexicon warped, and Ashtray Rock fell into parlance, too. Plaskett called it by that name as early as 1998, when he mentioned the place on the Thrush Hermit rarity "Tired and True." It became a "cliché suburban hangout spot," Benvie says — just far enough into the woods to avoid adults, just close enough to home, just proximate enough to a McDonald's.

It was the perfect place to smoke and drink, if that was something you did. Plaskett didn't; he was more comfortable as sober observer — a role he relishes even today, preferring, usually, to soak in the moment rather than soak in booze. It was Benvie, who occasionally ran with another circle of friends, who was more prone to spending teenaged weekends drinking and smoking in those woods. But as Plaskett mulled the idea of a high school–centric rock opera, it became clear that Ashtray was the perfect setting. It was technically in suburban Halifax, but it could have been anywhere — the city, the country, wherever kids wanna make noise.

And so Plaskett began to build a story around those feelings and memories. In the contexts of high school and heartbreak, he was able to find a place for unreleased songs stretching far back into his career. He'd demoed "Nothing More to Say" as an acoustic number with Bob Hoag in Arizona. "Drunk Teenagers," originally demoed in 2003 and set on the road halfway to Thunder Bay, was molded into an introduction to *Ashtray Rock*, both the record and a place: no matter how far you feel from the rest of the world, there are like-minded kids out there who want to do the same things. He'd originally recorded "The Glorious Life" in 1995 with Thrush Hermit, having written the once-speedy song after dropping off Kraatz at the airport from the "French Inhale" video shoot. "Ashtray Rock," the song, is an adaptation of

Plaskett and Gordie Johnson recording *Ashtray Rock* in 2006. [© Dave Marsh]

"When You Failed English," a Thrush Hermit demo from the same era, originally full of Sloan-inspired localisms, including the numbers of the buses Plaskett & Co. would take to get downtown. The Hermit had fooled around on "Snowed In," too, and Plaskett did a rough demo for it with the Emergency in 2003.

The Emergency returned to Phase One in Scarborough to record the album in late 2006. Three-quarters of the songs were fully written and practised before they had arrived, affording them time in the studio to play with the music's heaviness — a Gordie Johnson specialty — and tempo. The *Globe and Mail* described the record's sound as "Elvis Costello transplanted into a Canadian garage band," but the songs that follow harness a far wider range of influences. After opening with a snippet of "Soundtrack for the

Night," Plaskett indulges in what Johnson lovingly calls a "great moment in guilty guitar binging," using his Gibson RD and a phase shifter to push the studio speakers like they're Marshall cabinets. "Drunk Teenagers" takes musical cues from "The Interpreter," a 1977 psych-rock song from reclusive Austin musician Roky Erickson. The double groove of "Snowed In/Cruisin'" could be two separate Stones songs, if Tom Petty took the mic halfway through. "Penny for Your Thoughts" references early Motown and rock 'n' roll, nodding to Rebecca Kraatz's preferred tastes in music. And on "The Instrumental," Kraatz's own voice is beamed in from the Mullet in Halifax, reading a fictional postcard while Gordie Johnson pays tribute to one of her favourite songs, Santo & Johnny's "Sleepwalk," on lap steel. As the song's breakdown comes to a close, Dave Marsh channels his best Keith Moon, hammering out the record's climax.

Marsh and new Emergency bassist Chris Pennell recorded their parts in less than a week, leaving Plaskett and Johnson behind to tie up the record. "Fashionable People" emerged after the rest of the band left, and sounds distinctly different from the rest of the record — in part because it borrows far more inspiration from Jurassic 5's "Quality Control" than anything on classic-rock radio. He tried to push his ode to hip-hop even further by inviting Tone-Lōc to rap the third verse — but, unfortunately, his invitation went unheeded.

Plaskett went to great lengths to build the *Ashtray Rock* universe, singing from three different perspectives and getting Kraatz to illustrate a companion comic for the liner notes, as well as a matching album cover. The story's threads are pulled from everywhere, but the final narrative channels the excitement — and fragility — of playing music with your friends as a teenager. It takes listeners along the journey of two young bandmate protagonists — setting the scene, vomit and all, at an Ashtray Rock party, recalled from the nostalgic perspective of late autumn. Both bandmates fall in love with a mystery girl from out west, breaking up their band — and friendship — in the process. But in the midst of a wicked winter, the girl moves away, leaving both bickering bandmates behind. Reality sets in, maybe a little too late, as the bandmates realize that maybe they needed each other more than they needed her.

One recurring character in *Ashtray Rock* is, in fact, a real person: Dave Boyd, a metalhead who unsuccessfully ran for president of Clayton Park Junior High on the promise that he'd put a swimming pool beneath the floor of the school's gym. Plaskett transplanted Boyd into the record's fictional high school, turning him into a booze hookup. The campaign promise is there, too, bolstered by basketball and pool sounds recorded by McGettigan to run over the record's introduction. The final, hidden outro is a lament for the long-lost metalhead. Plaskett found Boyd's personality so brilliantly absurd that he even got Kraatz to recreate his junior-high yearbook photo for the back cover of the record, including the original caption: "Keep Metal Strong."* Boyd may be tertiary to the grander storyline, but his presence is

---

* Boyd has since run unsuccessfully for other political offices in Halifax. Now an occasional vlogger, he apparently accepted his role on the record with glee. Search the internet hard enough, and you can find a video of Boyd hiking to the actual Ashtray Rock.

a reminder of a constant in the Plaskett universe: you can always find reason to crack a grin, even after heartbreak.

MOST OF *ASHTRAY ROCK*'s borrowed stories can be traced back in some way to Benvie and McGettigan, and it's littered with inside jokes only they would get. In spite of their role in the narrative collage, though, Benvie and McGettigan have never really talked to Plaskett — or each other — about the record. "It's personal," McGettigan says with a laugh. "It's hard for me to lay out my exact take on it. It's different reflections on what Joel and I, Rob and I, Joel and Rob went through." While McGettigan suggests the kids on the album's cover might be Plaskett and Benvie, there are no salacious secrets about the history of Thrush Hermit to be gained from the record. Did a girl break up the band? Nope — everything a working band deals with *except* girls did. Did they chase after the same girls as teenagers? Well, maybe. "That's quintessentially high school," Plaskett says, chuckling, but even if it had happened, he insists it played little to no role in the Hermit's history. "You need to exaggerate to make good music. Most of it didn't happen. A record happened. It's fiction. But the inspiration is true. Even though I'm making plenty of music now that Rob and Ian couldn't care less about, their aesthetic and the sense of humour I had with those guys definitely informs my writing to this day." He points to the Hermit's other chief story-teller, Benvie, for comparison: "There are things in his last book, *Maintenance*, where I'm reading and going, 'That's in there for me and Ian.' Even if he's not consciously doing it, we're the only guys who are gonna know that reference."

It's less autobiographical narrative than autobiographical collage — an homage to the people, places, and moments in Plaskett's youth that shaped who he is today. The female protagonist's taste in music, for instance, is exactly the same as Kraatz's. And even when Plaskett bends the truth, there's still some to be found. After all, he didn't actually like Thrush Hermit's first two records on cassette — he can't stand *Nobody Famous*, because the (reasonably) high quality of the recordings plays up the band's confused direction and technical imperfections. But the cassettes' contents aren't what matters — it's the memory of making them, including the part where the band had to walk miles home from dubbing them in Burnside. "Part of what I love about music is it's a connection to a time in your life," Plaskett says. "So if you choose to document something, even if it's not the greatest song, the memory attached to it can be awesome. And that's more important than the song. Because if you keep that as the barometer for which you do things — 'This will be fun, this song, I just have to do it even though no one's gonna get it' — then eventually, if there's joy in that, somebody's gonna find it. They might not get everything you do, because there were things you did just for yourself that didn't strike them. But that entry point is gonna be there for people."

PLASKETT AND JOHNSON were absolutely giddy when they presented *Ashtray Rock* to the business team. For the second full-length in a row, Plaskett had thrown them a curveball.

"We just felt like kids getting away with something," Johnson says, "like we were great graffiti artists, and our great masterwork was illegal and ill-advised." The record was sprawling and complex — the opposite of a natural follow-up to "Nowhere with You." And its title was also more than a little confusing. Johnson remembers Sheri Jones standing with arms folded, questioning Plaskett: "How married are we to the title? Is it some kind of dance? Is it an actual rock?" Jones had grown up in west Halifax, too, and remembered escaping to the same woods as a teenager a few years before Plaskett and his friends did. Still, she says, "I thought it was ridiculous name." She and MapleMusic's Kim Cooke decided to let Plaskett follow his instincts. "Over time," Cooke says, "we got used to Joel doing this."

Ashtray Rock, released in 2007, served as the entry point for Plaskett's biggest audience yet, outselling even *La De Da*. While he lost the Best Songwriting Juno in 2008, "Fashionable People" went on to win the Billboard World Songwriting Contest. Writing in *Exclaim!*, former Halifax scenester Allison Outhit called the record "heartfelt and exuberant," "neither cynical nor earnest," and "an all-Canadian roman à clef." The *National Post* drew the obvious Springsteen parallel, with *Ashtray Rock* bringing Plaskett "closer than he's ever been to the icon who managed to romanticize a far less romantic place than Nova Scotia." Others called the album "absorbing, charming, entertaining, and moving" and "funny, smart, and heartbreaking."

Plaskett managed to tell a story that could resonate with any listener — and while *Ashtray Rock* could have been set anywhere, the fact that it lives and breathes Halifax helps make it a crucial addition to both his own body of work and to the legacy of great Canadian east coast music. The record marked the next step in the evolution of his post-Hermit career. He'd announced he was home on *Khyber*, called out the defectors with *Truthfully*, wrote Halifax a love letter on *La De Da*; here, he proclaimed his home's place in CanCon history.

The free-and-easy last days of high school, before the perils of adulthood, are universal within a certain socio-economic slice of North America. But for the many Plaskett fans who hail from Nova Scotia and the other Atlantic provinces, there's an added depth to *Ashtray Rock* because of the album's inextricable ties to geography. "This album just feels like home," wrote Halifax music critic Ryan McNutt. "No matter what path *Ashtray Rock* takes him on, Joel will always be Halifax's reliably brilliant talent; a reassuring thought, no less." For many, those last carefree teenage days are the last days spent on the east coast — at home — as the choices of adulthood force them to head west. By weaving loud-and-proud Halifax-isms into a classic story of high-school heartbreak, there's a relatability in the details that's absent from other Canadiana. The record is a booming announcement from a place where many voices go unheard: no matter where you're from, you still have a story to tell. You can still write the soundtrack for the night no matter how far removed you are from the rest of the world.

FOLLOWING THE RECORD, the Emergency's world got a little bigger. They took on a road manager, Stephen "Snickers"

Smith, and added a familiar fourth member on keys and guitar: Peter Elkas. He meshed well with the band, having played a handful of shows with them as early as 2005. The first incarnation of his Peter Elkas Band had even opened for the Emergency on a fateful 2003 tour where everyone in both bands got sick as dogs, leaving Plaskett and Marsh face down in their soup in Quebec on the way home from Kingston, Ontario's Grad Club. It took some time getting into a new routine with five people instead of three — frustrating Marsh, in particular — but it was a necessary adjustment. They embarked on a 2007 Canadian tour, eventually visiting the U.S. and even Australia again.

They ended the album cycle with a tour de force: six nights at Toronto's Horseshoe Tavern, to celebrate the storied venue's 60th anniversary. The band played an album a night, doing *Ashtray Rock* twice for good measure, to enthusiastic crowds. "It started off as just one night, and it grew into this great idea," says Horseshoe co-owner Jeff Cohen, who pitched the idea to Plaskett. "It was fun and exhausting," Plaskett says, "'cause we had to learn so much of the catalogue. It was good for the band, actually, to go back — really good for Chris, 'cause he didn't know a lot of that earlier material. But some of it was hard."

They equipped the residency with special guests — including Ian McGettigan, Rob Benvie, Bill Plaskett, Gordie Johnson, the Tragically Hip's Gord Downie, Sarah Harmer, Andrew Scott, and Tara S'Appart — and kept Elkas in tow to flush out the sound. Plaskett was used to providing the soundtrack for one night, but not six nights, and the residency forced him to reflect on the sheer size of

Plaskett onstage for the second of six nights at the Horseshoe Tavern in December 2007. [© Pete Nema]

his catalogue: "I've been going out and doing shows and there's not even a song from *Khyber* in them, let alone *In Need of Medical Attention*. It's hard for me to touch on all the records at this point, unless I want to play for three hours."

Marsh calls it "an honour" to follow in the footsteps of artists like Stompin' Tom Connors, who once played the Horseshoe for 25 nights straight. "It's only what I can imagine the Band went through in *The Last Waltz*," he says. "Not comparing ourselves to the Band, of course. It was just as exciting to be involved in it as actually doing it."

The Last Waltz, coincidentally, first came out as a triple record.

EVERY TIME YOU LEAVE

WITH ONLY FLEETING success on radio, touring has always been a necessary part of Joel Plaskett's career. He guesses his live show accounts for 60 or 70 percent of his livelihood. Those numbers mean he, like so many other Maritimers, has to hit the road to make ends meet. There's hardly enough population in the region to sustain a career by playing close to home, either, making tours a cumbersome commitment. The closest major music market is Montreal, a 14-hour drive from Halifax. Even if he flies, gigs away are either expensive, a long slog, or both.

His diverse repertoire, at least, offers him lots of flexibility. His growing volume of solo material gives him the financial opportunity to play shows alone when he can't afford to take the Emergency. This, of course, can be a strain on the band, whom Plaskett would rather keep distant than disappoint: "I can't ask the guys in my band to go have a tour and not get paid." His incessant touring is also something his wife, Rebecca Kraatz, has gotten used to over the years. "I've always been good at doing things alone," she says. And over time, being away from home got tougher on Plaskett himself. By 2008, he'd spent more than half his life playing music, much of it on the road. Tours felt longer, destinations got further. "If you want to feel far away from home, go to Australia," Plaskett says. "I really like travelling, but I gotta say, it takes it out of me."

But since making music is the only thing he's ever wanted to do, when it pays, he plays. Breaking into new markets has never been easy for Plaskett, especially after the nightmare that followed *Sweet Homewrecker*. "I just feel happy that I have a cool career in Canada, and I can go out and play to people who care," he says. "I'm still reaching people, but I don't need it to feel like it's international." When he tried Australia, he didn't just feel far from home — he found himself too often playing to over-excited Canadian expats, making it difficult to win over locals. The U.S., meanwhile, has always been supersaturated with its own artists, making it financially risky to tour — unless he's alongside a larger act like the Tragically Hip, who themselves have long struggled to get much attention outside the confines of Canada. Save, perhaps, for the hip-hop artist Drake, Americans — who represent the world's largest music market — tend to reject artists who both stay in Canada and embrace their heritage in song. "I've pretty much given up on the States, unless I get offered a bulletproof opportunity," Plaskett says. One of those opportunities, in February 2008, was the Folk Alliance International Conference in Memphis.

THE FOLK ALLIANCE would best be described as a mutual admiration festival — it exposes like-minded artists and industry types to each other as they network, mingle, and play for one another for nights on end. In 2008, Plaskett went down with Sheri Jones and a handful of Halifax musicians, including David Myles and Rose Cousins. The festival tends to take over whole floors of the host hotel; on the Friday night, as a party spilled into the hallway, Plaskett got chatting with Ana Egge, a Brooklyn-via-Saskatchewan songwriter and a friend of Cousins. They talked about soul music, and after someone interrupted their conversation, Plaskett started singing one of Egge's songs to her. "I was like, 'Wait a minute — *who are you?* How do you know my music?'" she recalls, laughing. It turned out they had a mutual friend — Peter Elkas — who'd turned each of them onto the other's music. Plaskett, Egge says, "had my attention right away." After a while, he extended an offer: he was going into a local studio the next day — would she want to come in to hang out, and maybe sing some harmonies?

That studio belonged to Doug Easley, the *Sweet Homewrecker* producer who Plaskett had last seen on his long drive to Arizona to make *La De Da*. He'd tried to book time with Easley during the previous year's Folk Alliance, only to find out his original studio had burned down. When Plaskett arrived in 2008, he called Easley up and found out he'd gotten a new space. "Cool," Plaskett told him. "You got any time on Saturday?" It turned out he did — and, after roping in Cousins and Egge, he stopped by to record.

In concert, Plaskett had been toying with a travelling song called "Wishful Thinking," and he decided to put it to tape at Easley's. It wasn't fully written, though, so he decided to wing much of it, making up new verses as he went along. He gave some of the lines to Cousins and Egge and got them to play around with their vocals — "He-heee" here, "Hoo-hooo" there — as he listened in amazement at their combined voices. The awe was reciprocated, Egge says: "He's got boundless energy and so many things coming to mind."

After an afternoon of messing around in the studio, the crew had recorded more than seven minutes of material, creating a trundling track that feels like a journey down the endless Trans-Canada Highway. It was mixed by the end of the day, and Plaskett made everyone go into his car to listen to it before they left. It was a fun, if baffling, tune. "'Wishful Thinking' is not a conventional song in any way," Cousins says. "How does that even fit on a record? Let alone stand up as a song on its own? But that's what's easy to love about it."

Having been on the road with the Emergency most of the last year, Plaskett wanted to spend 2008 decompressing. Still, he was toying with the idea of recording *something*. Later at the conference, Plaskett was having a drink with Sheri Jones and David Myles when he made an off-the-cuff joke — wouldn't it be funny if he made a triple record? Jones didn't take it lightly. She'd been working on plans to build an audience for him in the U.K., but a triple record would be impossible for new fans to digest. She stayed up all night wracking her brain over how to deal with such a project, only to later hear from Myles that Plaskett was just trying to annoy her, and that he'd succeeded.

But when he gets an idea in his head, it's hard to shake it out.

PLASKETT HAD RECENTLY rented a small building — more of a shack, really — in downtown Dartmouth, which he turned into a studio. In honour of Nova Scotia, he called it Scotland Yard. There, on his old eight-track tape machine, he recorded a few songs for acts like Yellow Jacket Avenger and Peter Elkas. In April, just months after the Folk Alliance, Plaskett visited Calgary for the Juno Awards, where he ran into Ken Friesen, a recording engineer who'd worked with the Tragically Hip, Hawksley Workman, and the Sadies. Friesen told him about a 16-track tape machine he'd heard was for sale in Toronto, and Plaskett decided he needed to have it. By the start of May, the 16-track had arrived in Dartmouth, and Friesen came down to help him wire it.

Plaskett suddenly had a serious studio. He didn't feel like taking a break anymore — he had music to make.

He loved the way Cousins and Egge sounded together, and began to think about bringing them in for a record. "Wishful Thinking" made him want to wing it, making up whole parts for an album as he went along. So he called the girls up, and they convened at Scotland Yard, along with another guest: his father.

Some of the songs Plaskett was composing leaned more toward Celtic-influenced, "Maritime"-sounding traditional folk than much of his previous work. These were Bill Plaskett's specialties, making him an obvious fit to help out.

Bill and Joel Plaskett in the original Scotland Yard studio.
[© Ingram Barss]

His dad also happened to be great at finger picking, which Plaskett was considering writing into some songs. Not that he needed a particular reason to involve the man who'd first taught him guitar, of course. "I just thought it would be cool, to be honest," Plaskett says. "It just made sense. He's been really supportive, and I thought, 'Here's an opportunity to do something in a studio close to home, so I can involve people close to home.'" Bill felt honoured to be involved, both proud to be there and fascinated to be able to watch his son work on such an ambitious project. "Long story short," the elder Plaskett says, "I've got a lot to learn from him at this stage of the game."

In naming his new songs, Plaskett started playing around with the number three. It was, after all, shaping up to be his third solo record, and he happened to be 33. When he was working on "Gone, Gone, Gone," which he partly recorded with Ian McGettigan in Toronto, he thought about doing a whole record of songs with triple-barrelled names. But he started churning out such a high volume of music that neither that naming system, nor the trappings of a conventional album, really made sense anymore.

"I was like, 'How am I gonna put them all on there?' And then I was like —" Plaskett emulates his best stoner voice "— *Three*." He bursts out laughing. "It sounds dumb, but it was literally that."

His off-the-cuff joke about a triple record had become a feasible reality. There aren't a whole lot of triple records out there, and he saw this as an opportunity to do something original while, in a small way, joining the ranks of classic triple LPs like the Clash's *Sandinista!* and George Harrison's *All Things Must Pass*. He also felt, of course, that the pile of songs he'd written merited official release.

Going for a triple record was a decision that didn't particularly shock Plaskett's collaborators. "He doesn't have anything that stops him," Cousins says. "He just comes up with an idea and he's like, 'I'm gonna do this, it's gonna be great.' It's not necessarily reckless abandon, but it kind of is. He doesn't have any inhibitions."

Sequencing the nearly 30 tracks was another ordeal. Putting all the "Word, Word, Word" songs on a single disc wouldn't work if the other two discs didn't have a consistent theme. When Plaskett started to look at the songs lyrically and thematically, though, and a pattern started to appear. "There were these songs about leaving, these songs about being alone, these songs about coming home," he says.

"That kind of gave me the structure for the record — where I composed it like a journey."

Journeys were on his mind: touring behind *Ashtray Rock* for months on end, as far away as Australia, had left him exhausted. Making a triple record was its own long road, too. "I know it's super conceptual," he says, "and could be very easy to deem pretentious. But it made sense for me to structure it in a way that felt like a journey. Because if you're going to have people even tune in for that long, which is unlikely — I'm sure most people don't listen to it as a triple in one fell swoop — I liked the idea that it would be a three-act play."

As he got older, he was thinking less about the excitement of touring and more about who he was leaving behind — namely his wife, Rebecca. He began to dream up songs from her viewpoint as the record developed, exaggerating the perspective, much like he did with *Ashtray Rock*. "When you're travelling all the time, it's easy to be like, 'Oh, I'm doing my thing,' and one year literally blurs into the next," he says. "But when you're the person who's at home, the environment is considerably more static, and you don't have company — suddenly it's a little less romantic. Travelling in itself, around the world, or touring, is a romantic notion for people — *Yeah, I drove down to Arizona* — it all looks good on paper. But there is a flipside to that, which is that somebody's home, if you have a partner. That's probably why, for a lot of musicians, their marriages break up. It's not an easy lifestyle, because you're getting all this stimulation and yet you may have somebody who's home. It's not like Becky was sitting there waiting for me by any stretch of the imagination, but she's not a big traveller. But when I get home, the idea of going somewhere alone is an exhausting prospect."

As the summer of 2008 rolled along, Plaskett spent endless days and nights recording, sweating away hot days in a tank top as his father, Egge, Cousins, and a slew of other guests came in to record various parts. They shaped a sound that differed vastly from the rest of Plaskett's catalogue, steeped in more influences than ever, bridging rock, pop, country, soul, and folk. "He's constantly feeding the listener and the fan in himself," Cousins says. "I really love that about him. He's not precious —" she pauses to laugh "— precious, precious about setting himself apart."

The sessions produced a three-act record that serves as a dialogue between Plaskett the traveller and the love he leaves behind. On the first disc, he hits the road, somewhat begrudgingly; "Through and Through and Through," the Matthew Grimson cover "Drifter's Raus," and "Wishful Thinking" are the traveller's songs.* Meanwhile, the lover watches him walk away in songs like "Every Time You Leave," the Irma Thomas cover "Wait, Wait, Wait," and "Gone, Gone, Gone." The first disc ends with "Run, Run, Run," which Plaskett likens to a Greek chorus mixed with the traveller's final pleas: will you meet him when he returns?

In the more complicated second act, the traveller floats along the road alone. "Safe in Your Arms" is a

---

*   Plaskett had always liked "Drifter's Raus," written by his friend and mentor Matthew Grimson years earlier, but it was never properly released. "He really liked it," Grimson says, "possibly more than I did, because he was determined to get it out there."

down-on-your-luck follow-up to Thrush Hermit's "The Day We Hit the Coast," with a sly hat-tip to Cormac McCarthy's book *The Road* — you can set out on a journey, he sings, but the pot of gold you were told is at the end of the rainbow isn't usually there. "Shine On, Shine On, Shine On" takes the lonesome traveller to Australia, while the lover left behind returns for "Sailor's Eyes" — a song that, along with "Pine, Pine, Pine," is among the most explicitly Maritime-style folk songs of Plaskett's career. Act Two gets darker as it leads up to "Beyond, Beyond, Beyond," a song that steps outside of *Three*'s perspective and into Plaskett's real life, about one of his oldest family friends from Lunenburg who was killed in a murder-suicide. "I don't sing it that often," he says. "I have to be in the right frame of mind where people are listening. But really, I think it's one of the best songs I've ever written, because I think it strikes the tone that I wanted with it."

The darkness sticks around in "Demons," written in the late '90s for a friend struggling with mental illness. Act Two ends with Plaskett's traveller looking back toward home for "New Scotland Blues," written before the rest of the record at a time of year Plaskett's songs regularly revisit: as the autumn's last big storm comes in, whipping up the weather just before winter. The song is soft, but the traveller's angsty: after spending a year on the road playing for others, all he wants to do is get back to playing music for himself. Here, he says, the feelings are real. "With this record, it's probably my most personal statement as far as an album goes."

The dialogue returns in *Three*'s final act, with help from Cousins and Egge, either as voices from above ("Rewind, Rewind, Rewind") or the lover back home ("Precious,

Precious, Precious"). There are tracks about dropping everything ("Lazy Bones"), straight-up love songs ("All the Way
Down the Line"), and one last travelling number for good
measure ("Rollin', Rollin', Rollin'"). The twelve-and-a-half-
minute "On & On & On" caps off the record: a party jam
with the whole gang in tow.

Plaskett invited Chris Pennell and Dave Marsh to
Scotland Yard to record the song's backing track, whispering
instructions for them into the microphone as he played verse
after verse and improvising as the song went along. Later
on, Plaskett taped the mountain of lyrics to a blanket on the
studio wall, and Cousins and Egge came in for what would
be their final vocals for the album. The three used a single
mic, leaning in when it was their turn to sing, occasionally
ad libbing. To set the mood for the party jam, they passed
around a bottle of Jameson; listen closely, and you can hear
the cap screwing off and on. The vocals on the song are
almost entirely from the first take, save for a few fumbled
lines that were re-recorded, and the mic gets more and more
distorted as the song goes on, and on, and on. The track is
loaded with references to the rest of the album; to Plaskett's
life, friends, and family; to the late Halifax visual artist and
Quahogs singer Scott Tappen; even to Canadian icons
Stompin' Tom Connors and Shelagh Rogers. At the end of
the road, though, is White Fang — the stray, deaf cat with a
Jack London-referencing name that he and Kraatz adopted
on September 11, 2001, to do something good in the world.

Ending with White Fang, Plaskett says, completes the
song cycle. "To me, that cat was like coming home — no
slight on Rebecca," he says. "You come into your house, you

see your cat eating the same thing it ate the day you left. That's how you know you're back."

THE RECORD CONSUMED Plaskett for the whole summer. When Nova Scotia rapper Classified, a fan of "Fashionable People," suggested they collaborate, Plaskett wrote a hook inspired by his obsessiveness over the sessions — leading to a song called "One Track Mind." As he worked on *Three*'s aesthetic, Plaskett's obsession continued. Crack the record open and you'll see White Fang sleeping in the bass drum at Scotland Yard as Plaskett looks on, his whole world organized in triplicate: guitars, tape reels, snare drums, mixing board faders, plugs in the floor. "I went as far down the wormhole as I could," he says. "I lost my mind doing it, but it was pretty fun." The Persian Kilim rugs he'd draped along the walls of the studio, meanwhile, would go on to serve as the album's main art, his face superimposed on top. He used one rug for the CD and another for the vinyl edition. *Three* would be the first full-length vinyl record to come out on New Scotland Records, an imprint he started in 2008 to give his projects physical releases, with the now-deceased White Fang as its logo. (RIP, little buddy.) Plaskett followed it up quickly with a seven-inch of outtakes dubbed *Three More*. "I just like the idea of creating things and having a lasting physical product that exists outside of an MP3 on the internet," he says. "I wanted to create a vinyl collection for myself as much as anybody else."

Plaskett didn't show his management anything from *Three* until it was done. His manager Sheri Jones was surprised at the delivery: "It went from, 'I'm gonna start on my record' to 'Here's my triple record; what do you think?'" Marsh and Pennell, too, were unaware that Plaskett was recording a full album, despite playing the rhythm track for "On & On & On." "We didn't know what we were recording for, and he didn't tell us," Marsh says, "and the next thing you know there's a triple album." As he usually did, the drummer had been filling in the time between Emergency projects by doing home renovations around Halifax. He was frustrated to be left out again, but had found another venue to make music, releasing his debut solo record, *The True Love Rules*, in the summer of 2008. Pennell, meanwhile, played around in other bands and decided to go to hairdressing school so he could take shifts at his girlfriend's salon rather than return to taxi driving. "When I joined the band, it was no secret to me that there was gonna be the folk-world kinda thing going on," Pennell says. "The way I deal with it is I try to occupy my time with other musical things." But he doesn't commit too much. "I keep my priority playing with the guys."

Plaskett unleashed *Three* in Canada in March 2009, and it became the best-selling record of his career, going Gold within six months. "He expects a lot from his fans — for people to go along with him on these adventures," says Tara Luft Mora, who handled much of his marketing and promotion at MapleMusic. "He hasn't taken a wrong turn yet." The record finally snagged Plaskett a Juno — the conspicuously titled Adult Alternative Album of the Year — after five nominations since the end of Thrush Hermit. In *Exclaim!*, Vish Khanna called it focused in spite of its sprawl and "simply a great reminder of Joel Plaskett's singular talent and gutsy artistic drive." Other critics said the record was "ambitious, but it doesn't overreach" and "a spell of personal storytelling, easy-breezy harmonies, and Westerbergian rock." Montreal's *Hour* called it a new CanCon classic, and in the Fredericton *Daily Gleaner*, a critic wrote that "Plaskett is incredibly gifted, incredibly prolific, and incredibly true to himself as a musician. *Three* proves this again — and again — and again."

Soon after the album's release, Plaskett gathered together a core crew — Cousins, Egge, his father Bill, and tour manager Snickers — and hit the road. It was a major shift in presentation: one to four people onstage at a given time, playing less raucous material than the Emergency, but with more energy than the *La De Da* era solo shows. They played theatres instead of bars, cafes, or smaller rooms. "I'm sure people who really wanted the rock show might not have been as into it, but it also opened up the door to a wider audience," Plaskett says.

The crew played a handful of gigs across the Maritimes in April, then began their westward trek in Cobalt, Ontario. The packed crowd in the old mining town north of North Bay blew Cousins away — "There was a group of, like, 10 kids who had driven eight hours to see him. And they had made T-shirts [that looked like] the carpet from the cover." The enthusiasm carried on through May as they continued their trek. "I had never performed to an audience where there's so much genuine love," Egge says. "You'd hear young men yell out, 'I love you, Joel!'"

Plaskett was the headliner, no doubt, but he let Cousins and Egge take centre stage for a song every night. Bill

Plaskett got to step out from his son's long shadow, too. The "classic" cross-Canadian road tour, he says, rejuvenated him. "It was an affirmation of my own music, in a way, with the affirmation coming from my son, as well as from audiences who appreciate it. What more could you ask for?"

DURING THE *THREE* cycle, Sheri Jones got her wish about building a U.K. audience for Plaskett while solving the triple-album conundrum. He flew there four times in the course of a year, supporting a compressed *Three to One* CD released exclusively for that market. He played shows there in various configurations with Elkas and Egge, even recording a track, called "When I Go," with the pair at Abbey Road's Studio Two. But that wasn't the only historic place Plaskett played in 2009.

Working with Horseshoe Tavern promoters Jeff Cohen and Craig Laskey and his longtime agent Tom Kemp, Plaskett booked a concert at Massey Hall to end the cross-Canada tour. He nearly sold out the 120-year-old Toronto venue, which has hosted iconic concerts by the likes of Neil Young and Gordon Lightfoot. Plaskett roped in the Emergency and Peter Elkas for the final few dates of the tour in Ontario, including the Massey show. If ending the *Ashtray Rock* tour cycle with six nights at the Horseshoe was a sign that Plaskett had made it in Canadiana, Massey signalled his intention to sustain that momentum. It was a fitting end to a tour supporting his most ambitious record to date. *Three* was about the struggles of the touring musician, the long slogs far from home to make the career worth it — the risks required

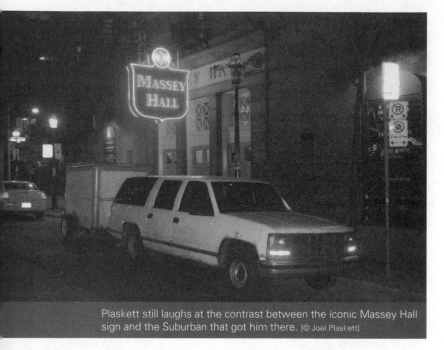

Plaskett still laughs at the contrast between the iconic Massey Hall sign and the Suburban that got him there. [© Joel Plaskett]

to squeeze out the rewards. In the end, he was rewarded by playing in one of Canada's most storied concert venues.

"That was one of our best gigs, for sure," Plaskett says, with far more reservation than the band he assembled for the show. "Everyone was on such a high," Egge says. "There was so much love and energy." Peter Elkas calls it "an amazing experience. Not everyone would do that kind of thing — extend [Massey Hall] to everyone they know. But that's the kind of thing Joel would do. He would want it to be a family thing and have everyone involved."

"It was a turning point for him," remarks Tom Kemp, who'd by then been booking shows for Plaskett for nearly a decade. "I remember standing sidestage just before he was about to go on, with him and his dad, Bill — looking

The band at Massey Hall: Joel Plaskett, Ana Egge, Peter Elkas, Chris Pennell, Bill Plaskett, Dave Marsh, and Rose Cousins.
[© Stephen "Snickers" Smith]

through the crack and seeing the audience, and thinking, *This is so far removed from where we started*. For him to be up on that stage was an amazing moment. Everybody who was on the periphery paid attention at that point."

Everybody, it turned out, included a Beatle.

TWENTY-SIX THOUSAND PEOPLE showed up to the Halifax Common on July 11, 2009, for a chance to see Sir Paul McCartney. Bands across the country were jumping over each other to convince the show's promoter to let them open for him, but McCartney's management had already hand-picked their openers: Winnipeg songwriter Sierra Noble, Halifax-turned-Montreal band Wintersleep, and the Joel Plaskett Emergency.

Naturally, Plaskett was nervous the day before the show. He felt a cold coming on, but he'd sung his way through plenty of those before, so he took some Advil and tried to catch some sleep. He was jarred awake at 3 a.m. to the sound of a fight breaking out in the street — and, when he looked out his window, he saw a man lying motionless. He rushed out to see what happened. The man had been beaten, badly, with a beer bottle; Plaskett immediately called 911. The victim was rushed to hospital and survived. Plaskett, meanwhile, wound up giving police statements until 6:30 a.m., at which point he had to drag himself across the Halifax harbour to load gear in for the biggest concert of his career.

As the day wore on, he started to feel a little bit better. For the occasion, he'd invited most of the same cadre of friends that had played with him at Massey, including Marsh, Pennell, Elkas, Cousins, and Egge. But just before the band was about to soundcheck — and then, maybe, have a chance encounter with McCartney — a huge boom echoed across the Common.

All of the generators on site went down.

Tech staff worked on the generators for 20 minutes, eventually fixing the problem. But it meant they were behind schedule. A staff member approached Plaskett: "You're on." No time to think, no time for introductions — "Just go," Plaskett recalls. He ran onstage to the mic to test it: "Is this thing on?" His voice rattled over the PA, answering his own question. As the band scrambled to get their monitors ready, Snickers shoved every fader on the sound board to the max. Plaskett counted down: four, three, two, one. A wall of sound washed over the Common, followed by Cousins and Egge's voices: "Through and through and throooouugh."

It'd been a decade since Thrush Hermit had imploded, leaving Plaskett to start from scratch. But here he was, opening for Paul McCartney in front of tens of thousands of people, still playing by his own rules: surrounded by friends onstage, making music the way he felt like it, refusing to compromise. Getting there wasn't a coming-home story — it was a staying-home story of incessant hustle nearly 20 years in the making. It took a lot of long journeys, but Plaskett wouldn't have it any other way. "I feel lucky that it didn't accelerate, 'cause there's less to come down from," he says. "You run the danger of it going to your head in a different way when it accelerates, especially when you're young. So I feel like it's been a blessing, in many respects, the slow build of my career."

Two weeks after the McCartney concert, an email appeared in Plaskett's inbox addressed to three people: Ian McGettigan, and Cliff Fenwick Gibb, and him. It was from Rob Benvie.

TIME FLIES

"MAYBE IT'S THE heat melting my mind," Rob Benvie began his email. "I'm in India for the summer, where it's pretty ruthlessly hot and it gets to you after a while."

He was there working on his second book, *Maintenance*, and had been looking through his iTunes library when he came across "Strange to Be Involved," a song about unrequited efforts and unresolved circumstances that he'd written for *Sweet Homewrecker*. "It struck me," his email continued, "that if we are ever going to follow through on any long-imagined Hermit reunion show(s), this winter would be the time. Ten years after and all that."

Since they parted ways in December 1999, Thrush Hermit's members had occasionally collaborated — Benvie and McGettigan in Camouflage Nights, McGettigan and Plaskett in the Emergency, and various other combinations for one-off gigs in Halifax and Montreal. Nothing serious, though. But in 2009, Benvie put forward the idea of a serious reunion. "It's funny," he says now. "As much as I was the instigator of our breakup, it was me who set it in motion."

Anything that happened would require finding gaps in four very busy schedules — writing, touring, producing, and day jobs would get in the way. They also had to decide how it would play out. The four members began to exchange calls and emails. They had a lot of questions to answer: on what scale could they make something happen? Would they release new songs? Re-release old ones? Would people care? Would they come to shows?

"I'm sure we all have our own individual visions," Benvie's email concluded, "but I think there's a way we could do it that would be classy, potentially lucrative, and most importantly fun."

Enough people got involved in the conversation that rumours began to swell. In December, Plaskett confirmed to media that the band would reunite for a handful of shows in New Brunswick, Nova Scotia, and Ontario. The plans soon ballooned. At Christmas, Benvie went over to Plaskett's in Dartmouth, and they talked about what to release with the tour. "I think we'd had a few whiskeys, and we kind of just decided, *Let's put everything out*," Benvie says. "Let's just put every single thing we've ever recorded out as a box set, kinda knowing it would be a money loser, but the die-hards would appreciate it. And so that's what we did. We were always ambitious dudes, and this release thing spiralled out of control."

The band announced a box set, *The Complete Recordings*, in February. Save for a few loose recordings Plaskett found later — like a bootleg of a show at CBGB's in New York — the box set compiled nearly everything, from early singles on Bong Load and Genius to a sound collage of the band's first junior-high recordings as Nabisco Fonzie. "If I wanna put my '90s self in a box," Plaskett says, "this is it."

The classic lineup — Plaskett, Benvie, McGettigan, and Cliff Fenwick Gibb — set on a nine-date tour in March, including two sold-out nights at Lee's Palace in Toronto, bringing along their giant neon ROCK & ROLL sign, which McGettigan had kept for good measure. "Those were some of my favourite Thrush Hermit shows of all time," Cliff says. "I thought we were at the top of our game." Many were sold out, with both cult and new fans in attendance. They even held a third, all-ages show at Lee's Palace — opening their shows up to fans-turned-parents and, perhaps, a new demographic of supporters who would have been eight or younger at the time of the Hermit's demise. "It was thrilling, 'cause it was so many years later and they were all such good musicians," says their longtime manager Angie Fenwick Gibb. "It was seeing the Thrush Hermit I always knew they could be."

It was a one-off reunion, but it felt like a second chance, an opportunity to play music together unshackled from the expectations and discord that plagued their first run. The raw enthusiasm from fans old and new completely validated the mountain of effort the Hermit and their team had put in in the '90s. The members' paths had diverged wildly in the past decade, but getting back together felt natural. And they were tighter than ever. "We played better than we did back in the day," says Plaskett, who busted out his *Sweet*

Benvie, McGettigan, Fenwick Gibb, and Plaskett at Lee's Palace in 2010. [© Pete Nema]

Homewrecker era green gas-station uniform for the shows. "We were just all so much more relaxed and having fun, 'cause we were all friends again and excited about the fact that we were playing. It didn't have the same baggage as the last year the Hermit had." The members had done everything they could to make the band work in the '90s, says Benvie, and calling it quits "was a little sad." But the 2010 reunion, he says, "bookended it in a nice way that it wasn't sad at all."

BENVIE HAD BEEN among the throngs bemoaning the inflated major-label hype on Halifax in the mid-'90s, and he unknowingly predicted the bubble's end in a 1994 interview with MuchMusic. "It's more important murderecords or Cinnamon Toast Records exists," he said, "so that Halifax won't self-destruct once all the attention leaves — which it will." Some 16 years later, those specific local labels were dust, but his argument had long been proven right. Halifax's musical community was happy to thrive on its own. And so it was fitting that the Hermit's *The Complete Recordings* box set came out on Plaskett's New Scotland Records, a label somewhere near the centre of Halifax's new self-sustaining music ecosystem. Since its inception in 2008, New Scotland has reissued Plaskett's whole post-Hermit back catalogue on vinyl and put out a series of split seven-inches with artists like Shotgun Jimmie and Jeremy Fisher. It's also put out CDs and LPs for everyone from Dave Marsh, Al Tuck, and Peter Elkas to new faces like burgeoning Halifax songwriter Mo Kenney.

With his Scotland Yard studio, Plaskett planted his roots even more firmly in Halifax, shifting some of his work from the road to home as he produced records for Kenney, Two Hours Traffic, Jewel collaborator Steve Poltz, and New Brunswick's David Myles. Myles, a singer-songwriter who now hosts *The East Coast Music Hour* on CBC Radio in Halifax, had met Plaskett through Sheri Jones and began to get to know him better as they watched NBA playoffs at the same bar. They started discussing records and, fresh off *Three*, Plaskett mentioned he was getting more into producing. Some songs were exchanged, and soon Myles was in Scotland Yard recording his 2010 record *Turn Time Off*. "When he gets into something, he gets into it full-on,"

Myles says. "He really listens to what other musicians do, in terms of his production style, and rather than trying to focus on what makes it the same as other people, he really focuses on what's different. I think that goes hand-in-hand with his general philosophy about why he chooses to live here, why he chose to build his business here."

At the studio, Plaskett also wrote and recorded "On the Rail," an ode to Cape Breton's Cabot Trail, which became a finalist for CBC's Great Canadian Song Quest in 2009. In 2011, he gathered that song and others — demos, outtakes, and one-offs like the Abbey Road song "When I Go" — for the vinyl-and-CD collection *EMERGENCYs, false alarms, shipwrecks, castaways, fragile creatures, special features, demons and demonstrations.*

By then, it was clear that Plaskett was never satisfied with just releasing an album for the sake of an album. He had gotten used to fresh challenges: a road trip to a foreign studio in Arizona, a rock opera, a triple record. "I don't think I've ever heard Joel talk about an idea that didn't actually come to fruition," says Peter Elkas. This time, Plaskett found inspiration with "On the Rail," which he'd heard on CBC Radio the day after he'd completed it. The notion of writing an album's worth of songs, each on a deadline — rather than packaging them all together and waiting months for a finished product to come out — made for a fine new challenge.

Sheri Jones tried to talk him out of it, she says, "but the more I thought of it, the more I realized that it was such a cool idea." She got in touch with producers at CBC and commercial radio, and they bought into the concept, too. Soon, it was a done deal. The three-piece Emergency convened in Scotland Yard at the beginning of 2012 and began recording a song a week, documenting the process with YouTube videos.

The first song to emerge was "You're Mine," a twin to *Ashtray Rock*'s "Soundtrack for the Night" both in its theme — celebrating the joy of making rock 'n' roll — and in its lyrical nods to Hüsker Dü's "Pink Turns to Blue." They recorded nine more songs in the following weeks, including the Maritime anthem "Harbour Boys," which, too, lionizes making music, and "I'm Yours," a love song with more than a hint of autobiography. Never too far from a Plaskett project, Ian McGettigan lent his hands as an engineer for both "Tough Love" and "Time Flies." By March, the sessions finished with "Lightning Bolt," a six-and-a-half-minute anthem that would come to be the album's eventual opener and a concert staple.

A control freak by nature, Plaskett tends to dwell on the details of a song until they're perfected, but he couldn't do that this time. The record that sprung from these sessions, he says, "found its feet as it went along." Lyrically, he's quite happy with it — he doesn't consider a song finished until he's content with the words — but there are some songs, like "Slow Dance," that he walked away from too early to be 100 percent satisfied. Others, like "North Star" and "I'm Yours," have become personal favourites and live hits, and he's particularly happy with the lyrics for "Old Friends" and "Lightning Bolt," a pair of songs that approach life, aging, and adulthood from different angles.

When the weekly sessions were finished, Plaskett called up his manager to talk album art. He told her he wanted it to be the bust of Wayne Newton he planned to keep onstage

Chris Pennell demonstrating his elk-like strength with Dave Marsh after a 2012 Halifax concert. (© Craig Buckley)

with him on the subsequent tour. She relented, and an hour later he conveniently sent her another finished cover idea: a mechanical guitar-playing monkey. Jones remains convinced Plaskett was trying to fake her out, but admits "his weirdest ideas always work." On tour, he took that weirdness a step further. On top of the Newton bust, he brought along two of those monkeys, wired to a guitar pedal to dance on his command.

Plaskett called the album *Scrappy Happiness*, and released it in full later that spring. This time, his ambitions had an unexpected side effect. It only sold half as well as *Three* — in part, at least, because the individual songs had already been available so long on iTunes and CBC's website.

The Emergency playing in Halifax after the *Scrappy Happiness* release in 2012. [© Craig Buckley]

But the fast-and-loose recording tactic gave the album an energy that did not go unnoticed. The *Toronto Star* declared the "rough-around-the-edges" project a "summer-perfect" record, while the Halifax *Chronicle-Herald* couldn't help but point out its "unbridled joy."

AFTER RECORDING AND touring *Scrappy Happiness*, Plaskett started finding more joy at home. While his jaunts on the road still packed punch — he did another residency at the Horseshoe Tavern, this time for five nights — he'd gained a few reasons to hang around town more often. In the summer of 2012, he took possession of a building in downtown

Dartmouth with an old fur warehouse in the back and began to renovate it. The old Scotland Yard was a fine place for a studio, but it was rented — and, to be fair, barely more than just a shack. Here, New Scotland Yard was born: an expansive studio Plaskett could call his own, free for him to set up and use as he pleases. With it, he's built a reputation as a recording kingpin, working with his in-house studio engineer Thomas Stajcer to produce records for the likes of Mo Kenney and ex–Great Big Sea member Séan McCann. *Vice* has even called him "Halifax's Rick Rubin." David Myles, who recorded his 2014 album *It's Christmas* at New Scotland Yard, says the studio is part of a growing local infrastructure making the Halifax area better for musicians. "Hopefully, as things develop," he says, "it'll give people less reason to feel like they need to leave."

The professionally outfitted space lets him work on projects without always hitting the road — an option that's grown particularly important to him. In April 2011, he and Kraatz adopted a son, Xianing, from China. Parenthood has become a priority he's grateful for, but it's made him much more hesitant to leave home, especially for long stretches. Music has always been his life's passion, and Kraatz, he says, has always helped him keep that in the foreground. But with fatherhood, he's begun to reflect more on how he spends his days. He feels he owes time to his son and makes sure he gives it to him. "Adopting him and becoming a parent has definitely been the biggest challenge of my life, as well as put music into perspective in a way that I really enjoy," he says. "I feel that it's made me stronger."

Since he started spending more time at home, some

friends have taken to calling him the "Mayor of Dartmouth." He's hesitant to accept such a title, which might better belong to born-and-bred Dartmouth native Matt Mays, who immortalized the town in the song "City of Lakes." Still, he's become a well-known entrepreneur in its downtown, with neighbours regularly stopping him on the street to chat. In October 2015, he expanded his Dartmouth empire even further by opening the New Scotland Emporium adjacent to his studio on Portland Street. Shoppers can stop by and grab a coffee (courtesy of Dartmouth's Honey & Butter), pick up LPs (courtesy of Halifax's Taz Records), and give their hair a trim at Elk's Haircutting (courtesy of the Elk himself, Chris Pennell). It's the ultimate clubhouse, and a way to stay entrepreneurial without straying far from home. But on occasion, too, he gets beckoned to hop westward across the harbour to Halifax proper. In 2014, the Khyber Centre for the Arts was shuttered, in need of $4 million in repairs. Halifax's municipal council considered selling it, which likely would have seen the 19th-century Gothic Revival building torn down for new development. Plaskett became the face of the "Save the Khyber" movement, urging the city to conserve the heritage building where he met his wife and recorded his personal *Down at Muscle Shoals*. He showed up to the meeting where Councillor Waye Mason — another pop-explosion survivor, having founded No Records two decades earlier — tabled a 2,300-signature petition to ask the city to keep the Khyber. Councillors, joking about the local celebrity in their midst, voted to keep it under the city's stewardship. Its future still remains uncertain, but Plaskett has kept up his support, even when on the road, selling "I Met My Love Down at the Khyber" shirts to fans across the country with proceeds going toward the Save the Khyber movement.

FOR A FEW weeks in early 2014, an enormous poster of Plaskett's face was draped on the side of Ottawa's National Arts Centre, one of Canada's premiere performing arts venues. Having played twice with Symphony Nova Scotia in Halifax since 2006, he was invited to perform a one-night-only concert with the centre's house orchestra. The show, in April, nearly sold out. Backed by dozens of woodwind, string, and percussion players, the songs took on new lives: the growing tension of "Light of the Moon" exploded with timpani roars, and a chorus of basses and cellos turned "Lightning Bolt" thunderous. "I'm Yours" got slightly lighter accompaniment, but that didn't stop an audience member from proposing to his girlfriend during the tune, sending gasps, then claps, throughout the audience. The sound of an orchestra is always a force to be reckoned with, but Martin MacDonald, who conducted the evening, says "with an artist like Joel, who is larger than life onstage — the effect that it had was great."

Plaskett played a couple of new songs that night, including one he called "The Park Avenue Sobriety Test." It was a cheerful-sounding, call-and-response tune he'd been testing with audiences for a few months that had quickly turned into a crowd favourite. But darker themes run beneath the song's lighthearted exterior. Named after a smashed guardrail at the foot of a steep hill in Dartmouth, the song muses over lost chances and mortality. "You just don't know what you're going to get dealt," he told the Ottawa crowd as he began the song.

Death was on Plaskett's mind in 2014. Beloved Halifax musician Jay Smith, a member of Matt Mays's band El Torpedo, died a year earlier, just before the Emergency's final *Scrappy Happiness* show in Halifax. One of Dave Marsh's best friends and musical protégés, Tommy "Mugak" McGachy Smith, passed away a few months later. And Marsh himself had a brush with death in late 2013, when he waited too long to treat a bout of pneumonia and wound up with blood poisoning. "Things got pretty dark for 12 hours or so," the drummer recalls. He spent three days in the intensive care unit, leaving Plaskett terrified. "I've never seen someone so sick, and it put the fear in me, I'll tell you," the songwriter says. "All in all, it was a shit year. And a rough winter. A really, really long winter."

That heaviness weighed on Plaskett's next record, released in March 2015 on Kim Cooke's new label, Pheromone Recordings. *Joel Plaskett & The Park Avenue Sobriety Test*, like its title track, is a meditation on the many forces in life that can conspire against you. As he sings in the opener, "Illegitimate Blues," he can't help but feeling kinda fucked up; even if his life seems okay on paper, he's certainly worried about the world his son will inherit. Across 13 songs, there are laments about overdue rent, society's obsession with technology, even government phone surveillance, and he makes the case that the little frustrations in life can add up fast.

Plaskett, of course, can blend sorrow and optimism with surgical precision, and that approach guides much of the album. "Illegitimate Blues" casually references a depression of unknown origin, but it's a short enough song, he says, not to be taken truly seriously. The album's unnamed leading man dwells on the past because the present is too much to deal with ("On a Dime") and heads out the door ("Alright OK") only to lose his phone. There's an apology to the loved one left behind ("When I Close My Eyes"), a fight ("Credits Roll"), and, on "Captains of Industry," a sudden change of heart. The slow-drip centrepiece was partially inspired by Naomi Klein's 2014 book *This Changes Everything*, which explores the relationship between capitalism and climate change. Plaskett had started the song before reading the book, but Klein's perspective on activism fuelled the fire. The song marks an end to the stress of the album's first half with the recognition, Plaskett says, that everybody's on the same team. "You realize you're not at odds with each other; the world is at odds with you. Those pressures of living in a society with a lot of unfairness — if that weighs on your mind, it can make you an angry person."

From there, *Park Avenue* digs itself out of its hole: after a moment of sober reflection ("For Your Consideration"), there's a cover of Stephen Foster's "Hard Times," a 160-year-old traditional folk protest song with lyrics that still resonate with Plaskett today. It serves as a positive counterpoint to "Captains of Industry": "Hard times, come again no more." Three tracks later, Plaskett subverts his characters' melancholy on "Broken Heart Songs": "I didn't step to the mic just to tell you I'm down." The album-closing title track deals with darkness, too, but it's really about seizing the day. It's an acknowledgement that bad things are bound to happen, and what matters more is recognizing it's up to you to do something about it. "It sums up the theme," he says. "You're left to your own devices when you're walking home. And you can either choose to walk through this sketchy park at midnight or walk around it, but if you wanna get home you've gotta deal with it. At the end of the day, you've gotta deal with yourself."

The song's name was first coined by Plaskett's neighbour Roy Logan, who one day pointed out a smashed guardrail near two sharp turns as the musician walked home from his son's daycare. As city workers dragged it away, Plaskett recalls, Logan said, "That's the Park Avenue sobriety test." Plaskett admired Logan's subtle sense of humour; when the neighbour died a year later of cancer, just before the National Arts Centre show, his memorial was filled with laughter as guests shared his jokes and stories. Plaskett had toyed with other potential album names, including *Beyond the Frame* — a lyric that recurs throughout the album — as a way to acknowledge that friends can often struggle just outside of plain sight. But the memorial struck Plaskett. He wanted to give more meaning to Logan's one-off quip — a chance to give his sense of humour a second life. Soon enough, the phrase birthed both a song and an album.

A FEW BLOCKS from Park Avenue, at New Scotland Yard, Plaskett took a new approach to making *The Park Avenue Sobriety Test*, recording much of it live off the floor. It's studio as playground; just like *Clayton Park* was a portrait of the shredding live show of Thrush Hermit, *Park Avenue* captures the fun of Plaskett's performances 16 years later. With a cast of co-conspirators 20 deep, the record comes with a great sense of fun and improvisation. Gone is the radio sheen that coated his recordings since first joining forces with Gordie Johnson for *Make a Little Noise* in 2005. There are warts, goofs, and mic-checks. It's a kitchen party captured on tape.

"It wasn't like we rehearsed and got together," Plaskett says. "I sent some folks demos and went over the chords with a couple people here and there at different times. But a lot of it was, like, everyone showed up, we learned the song, and four hours later, usually, we had tracked it." Using *Scrappy Happiness* as a teachable moment, Plaskett forced himself and his crew not to linger too much on details. In doing so, the process became easier, more relaxed. Recording "For Your Consideration" late one night, for instance, "I was like, 'Let's mix it right now, because I don't know if I'll feel the same way tomorrow.'" There are impossible-to-recreate moments, like when one guitar is off by a semi-tone during the chromatic-climb climax to "Broken Heart Songs." You can hear Plaskett singing through a smile in the final lines that follow. "His continued pursuit of rock 'n' roll is essentially a chase for the joy found in that kind of giddy, adolescent moment," says Peter Elkas, who played on the song — and who insists is not personally responsible for the wrong notes.

The Emergency are on the record, and so are all their friends. "I love the space a trio creates," Dave Marsh says, but "when someone sits in with us, it's a cool new sensation." In fact, it's one for the Emergency history books: all three

Plaskett, McGettigan, Elkas, and Marsh at New Scotland Yard during the *Park Avenue* sessions. [© Dawny Negus Jr.]

bassists from the band's recording history appear, including Chris Pennell and Tim Brennan; Ian McGettigan doesn't play, but he shows up behind both the boards and the congas. Elkas is there, as is Charles Austin, a remnant of the five-piece days, and new keyboardist John Boudreau. Mo Kenney sings backing vocals alongside Erin Costello, who plays piano on the haunting "For Your Consideration."

"What stands out most for me is the bittersweet juxtaposition of the melancholy material and the joyous, gang-in-a-room approach to the presentation," Elkas says. "When I first heard the rough demos, I thought the songs were too emotionally down to suit the kind of production Joel had been talking about. Once we tracked a few of the numbers as the large, harmonious group, I realized that Joel probably knew that capturing and injecting that human connection would tie party balloons to a potentially sad and lonely kid." That's exactly the tone that Plaskett was going for. "Some people have told me they think it's my most melancholy record," he says. "I don't feel that way, because when I listen to it, I feel a lot of joy in the playing."

While he was working on the promotion for *Joel Plaskett & The Park Avenue Sobriety Test*, Cooke realized that as good as the record's name was, it was even more apt folded into an acronym: *Joel Plaskett & The PAST*. And it's true: on top of the career-spanning guest list, it's also the sound of a life's worth of influences wrung out on tape. There's the trad-folk passed down from his father, the hooks of Thrush Hermit, the blues-rock sensibility of the Emergency, and the solo reflection of projects like *La De Da* and *Three*. Zoom out on the album cover, and you'll see some familiar imagery scattered around New Scotland Yard: *Scrappy's* mechanical monkey, the rugs that inspired the covers of both *Ashtray Rock* and *Three*, and Rebecca Kraatz's original artwork for *In Need of Medical Attention* and *La De Da*. The acronym may have been incidental, Cooke says, but "it all ties together very, very well."

There is one key fixture from Plaskett's past missing from the record — his father, Bill, who was in Australia while the ragtag crew was recording in November 2014. But his traditional influence appears in parts of *Park Avenue*, nowhere more so than on "Hard Times," which Bill taught his son, and which they regularly play whenever they get a chance to share a stage. The trad-folk sound, which Plaskett has slowly embraced since inviting Bill to perform on *Three*, only enhances the album's kitchen-party feel. Rather than work within the confines of the distinctly Maritime-sounding genre, though, he challenges it, projecting his own vision onto the sound. Occasionally that comes by chance. J.P. Cormier's front-and-centre fiddle on "On a Dime," for instance, was originally recorded to harmonize with a banjo line — one that Plaskett muted once he realized how much he loved the fiddle alone. His taste, he admits, is subjective. "It's funny, because I love all that stuff, but it can get corny if it's approached the wrong way," he says. "When it feels right, it feels right. There's no other way to say it." Three decades after Émile Benoit scuffed his family home's floor at a folk festival after-party, Plaskett has come to embrace the music his father raised him on. It just took him awhile to make it work the way he wanted it to.

STUBBORNNESS RUNS THROUGH Plaskett's career. It's something Rebecca Kraatz learned very early on in their relationship. There's a story she'll always remember: as they were walking down the street in Toronto soon after they met, a friend asked him what, if he wasn't playing music, he'd do for a living. "Joel looked down, and said, 'I don't even want to think about that,'" Kraatz remembers. "It's like a thread that's pulled him all the way through to now." He's since executed this stubbornness in endless ways. Thrush Hermit scoffed at the major-label world; Steve Miller Band covers were cooler than conforming to expectations anyway. Concept albums are more interesting to him than radio hits. Even if it's triple the work, he sees no reason not to make a triple record. He even avoided making traditional east-coast folk music until he was sure he wouldn't sound corny.

In the past 25 years, this attitude has earned him an awful lot of admirers. Dave Marsh sees a little bit of Mick Jagger in his bandmate. "He's the London School of Economics kid who decided to take control of his destiny and make sure nobody fucked with him," he says. Early Emergency member Charles Austin, meanwhile, likes what Plaskett's shown the world: "He's definitely a good model of how you can be successful without being a dick. It's inspiring."

In documenting and nurturing the next generation of Halifax musicians, Plaskett's even filled the shoes Sloan left behind when they packed up murderecords and moved to Toronto in the mid-'90s. Since producing Mo Kenney's debut, he's regularly brought her along to open for him on tour — and, most recently, invited her to play guitar in his "Emergency Deluxe" touring band, where she can be seen trading riffs with Plaskett on songs like "Come On Teacher." "He's been instrumental to my career thus far," Kenney says. "It's nice to have someone like him supporting local music. He doesn't have to do that, but he does. . . . I still learn from him all the time. He's kind of my mentor."

People often ask Bill Plaskett if he's proud of his son — and of course he is. "But I'm also in admiration of him, in a way," he says. Joel's success "came about through a lot of dedication and mental focus and belief in himself — all of which are qualities that I admire. And so I'm pleased as punch that he has been able to sustain [his career] and grow it."

After booking shows at the Horseshoe Tavern and Lee's Palace in Toronto for more than two decades, Jeff Cohen has seen the biggest bands Canada has to offer. When Plaskett plays Toronto, the promoter can often be seen just off the side of the stage with a huge grin. He minces no words about Plaskett's performances: "I think the Emergency, with no offence to Blue Rodeo and other bands here, are the best rock 'n' roll band in Canada." Kind words aren't confined within Canadian borders, either. Clyde Lieberman, who discovered Plaskett in 1993 — now an executive in charge of music for shows like *The Voice* — calls him his "favourite of any artist with whom I have had the pleasure of working, period."

Plaskett's accolades continue to grow, too. The East Coast Music Awards keep stacking up, now two dozen high. In 2011, in the early days of streaming music, he became the first artist to reach a million on-demand plays on CBC's Radio 3 website. And three years later, he was handed Radio 3's Lifetime Achievement Award, for being a "true pioneer of the Canadian music scene." It was a vote of confidence, 21 years after he signed his first publishing deal with BMG as a scrawny teenager, in his commitment and contribution to the country's musical tradition.

Contrast that with the award he received from the readers of Halifax alt-weekly the *Coast* in 2002, on the heels of *Down at the Khyber*: Most Likely to Move to Toronto.* But rather than give into the pressure to move to Ontario, Plaskett continued to work in defiance of geography. After more than two decades of lessons learned and hype unheeded, Plaskett has largely opted not to follow music-industry

---

* He shared the award with Buck 65, who did, in fact, eventually move to Toronto — despite telling the *Coast* that he'd rather relocate to Madagascar than the Ontario capital.

expectations. "One of the things I often tell people who are from small places is 'You've got to move away from there,'" says Allison Outhit, the former Halifax musician who's now an executive at FACTOR in Toronto. "I probably would have given Joel exactly the same advice if I met him now, if he was a young performer: 'You have to get out of Nova Scotia, because there's just literally not enough people there for you to build your career.' Of course, I would have been wrong."

Plaskett took his career into his own hands, becoming an archetypal road warrior and building up a fan base that's as dedicated to him as he is to them. In doing so, he's never had to compromise in his music or his mailing address. "There was always enough money in it to make it worth leaving the house," he says. He calls himself lucky for coming up in the right scene at the right time, but when the hype on Halifax faded, he didn't give up on his dream. "Most people I know have some other idea of what they might want to do," he says. "To be honest, I have no backup plan. I have nothing else I could do. I've lived in a suspended adolescence since I was 18."

Plaskett is a big fan of regionalism — the celebration of local character, culture, and stories. That, to him, is true patriot love. And so he has fashioned himself as the regionalist-in-chief of a lovely, if regularly overlooked, corner of Canada. He does this with a healthy skepticism of how others expect him to behave: "Halifax, Nova Scotia, is the land of the free," he sings on *Park Avenue*'s "Alright OK," "I don't care what the anthem says." He doesn't need to be in Toronto, Montreal, New York, or Los Angeles to make music. He makes it on his own terms, crafting crucial Canadiana, roping in eager listeners regardless of where they're from with love letters to the east coast. His music, then, is a rare pop-culture phenomenon: a stubborn, acclaimed, against-the-grain take on the notion that you need to leave home to succeed in life. Why go away when you can go nowhere with him?

ACKNOWLEDGEMENTS

WRITING A BOOK first seemed like a lonely endeavour, but it only actually came together through the kindness of others. Jen Knoch championed this book from the moment I pitched it to ECW; she and Crissy Calhoun were infinitely patient and encouraging editors as the project grew and shifted forms several times. The book benefitted immensely from having another Plaskett fan, Laura Pastore, as its copy editor at ECW. Jacques Poitras, Carly Lewis, and Emma Godmere helped turn my initial ideas into a fully formed proposal. Matt Braga, Tom Henheffer, Kate Hopwood, Adrian Lee, and Sarah Ratchford each provided crucial feedback on various versions of the manuscript. Joanne O'Kane — Hi, Mom! — kindly spent her Christmas vacation helping proof the galleys. Chris Jones gave invaluable input on the opening chapter. Stephen Carlick and Kim Magi saved the day on the (too frequent) occasions when the Toronto Public Library's music periodical collection proved inadequate. After I spent months trying to settle on a title, Gabe Pulver pointed out that the best one had been in front of me the whole time. And my editors at the *Globe and Mail* were completely supportive when I said I wanted to write a book, even when I asked for a summer off to make it happen. Some material from my *Globe* reporting made its way into this book, too, and I'm thankful to have an employer that's cool with that.

Mark Mosher, Chris Webley, and Greg Lawson are responsible for much of my taste in music, and provided helpful criticism (and occasionally couches) as I researched and wrote. As this project stretched along, Kareen Sarhane, Tim Alamenciak, and the Maritime Mafia of Beaconsfield Village helped wherever they could, provided vital distractions, and unflinchingly subjected themselves to long rants about the stories I unearthed.

The bulk of this book was written in Toronto (ugh) with a pivotal draft rewritten in Verona, Ontario, and a few pieces assembled in Halifax, Miramichi, Vancouver, and Ottawa. The Toronto Reference Library made for a fine second home, but it wasn't as great as the apartment I scored on Airbnb, two blocks from the waterfront, to do interviews in Halifax in July 2014. Shoutout to all the ex–New Brunswickers in Halifax's North End — Brad, Sarah, Christian, Alison, Bun, Grady, and many others — who made the city feel like home with countless games of washer toss and trips to Gus' Pub.

This project would have been lacklustre, to say the least, without Joel Plaskett's time, enthusiasm, photos, contacts, and, most importantly, music. Thanks for everything,

Youthful Silver Child. Plaskett's manager, Sheri Jones, was nothing but helpful in arranging interviews and handling logistics, in spite of the weeks I spent hounding her by phone and email negotiating access. Ingram Barss, Greg Clark, Dave Marsh, Pete Nema, Joel Plaskett, Peter Rowan, Catherine Stockhausen, and Catriona Sturton dove into their archives and kindly let me reproduce photos and posters. (Individual credits for photographers and designers appear next to captions.) Kim Cooke provided album sales numbers. Mike Campbell provided great archival material, including a test pressing of *Ashtray Rock* that took the opening anecdote of chapter 2 full circle. More than 50 people lent their time for interviews for this project, and many of them spent months fielding fact-checking emails as I cross-referenced information. Rob Benvie, Ian McGettigan, and Marsh were the chief recipients of these questions and responded keenly. (Marsh, for the record, makes for a formidable ally at Celtic Corner trivia.)

Thanks to my father, Mick, who introduced me to Clapton, Zeppelin, and the Wilburys, and taught me to never stop hustling; and to my mother, Joanne, whose patience and grace with me, Jon, Joey — and Mick, too — was an essential lesson in endurance. If it weren't for people like them, the Maritimes wouldn't be a place to regret leaving.

NOTES

IN WRITING ABOUT Canadian music, I have been lucky enough to stand on the shoulders of giants. Michael Barclay, Ian A.D. Jack, and Jason Schneider did God's work in compiling *Have Not Been the Same: The CanRock Renaissance 1985–1995* (Toronto: ECW Press, Rev. ed., 2011). Two chapters in that text — "The Importance of Being Sloan" and "Never Mind the Molluscs" — were crucial to my understanding of the growth of alternative music in Atlantic Canada, and served as a strong foundation for my exploration of that scene in this book as it related to Thrush Hermit. To guide the trip through broader east-coast history in chapter 2, three volumes proved extremely helpful: Margaret R. Conrad and James K. Hiller's *Atlantic Canada: A History* (Toronto: Oxford University Press, 2010); S.A. Saunders's *The Economic History of the Maritime Provinces* (Fredericton: Acadiensis Press, 1984); and Donald J. Savoie's *Visiting Grandchildren: Economic Development in the Maritimes* (Toronto: University of Toronto Press, 2006).

This book relied primarily on original interviews to tell the story of Joel Plaskett, the Emergency, and Thrush Hermit. Unless noted in the text or sources section, all quotations were sourced from these interviews. They were conducted between May 2014 and May 2015, in Halifax, Toronto, and Ottawa, largely in person, occasionally by phone, and in several cases by email, Facebook message, and Twitter DM.

The following people were gracious enough to lend me their time for interviews and, in many cases, frequent fact-checking: Art Alexakis, Charles Austin, Mike Belitsky, Rob Benvie, Dave Bookman, Tim Brennan, Marc Brown, Mike Campbell, Greg Clark, Jeff Cohen, Kim Cooke, Stephen Cooke, Rose Cousins, Laura "Borealis" Hyde Crapo, Doug Easley, Ana Egge, Peter Elkas, Angie Fenwick Gibb, Cliff Fenwick Gibb, Jay Ferguson, Joe Fleischer, Carla Gillis, Brad Gooch, Matthew Grimson, Jim Henman, Bob Hoag, Darrell Johnson, Gordie Johnson, Sheri Jones, Steve Jordan, Tom Kemp, Mo Kenney, Rebecca Kraatz, Clyde Lieberman, Sebastian Lippa, Tara Luft Mora, John Angus MacDonald, Martin MacDonald, Sharon MacDonald, Colin MacKenzie, Dave Marsh, Waye Mason, Ian McGettigan, Dale Morningstar, Chris Murphy, David Myles, Mike Nelson, Allison Outhit, Chris Pennell, Bill Plaskett, Joel Plaskett, Benn Ross, Peter Rowan, Stephen "Snickers" Smith, "Miniature" Tim Stewart, Catriona Sturton, Jonathan Torrens, Everett True, and Al Tuck.

SOURCES

Unless noted here, all interviews are original.

1. AN INTRODUCTION

"I want to find a way to make it in Canada": Stuart Berman, "Thrush
Hermit Leader Finally Well Enough to Call It Quits — Band Set
to Part Ways after Years of Frustration," *Toronto Star*, December 2,
1999.

2. REWIND, REWIND, REWIND

"Maritimers, more than other Canadians": Harry Bruce, *Down Home:
Notes of a Maritime Son* (Toronto: Key Porter Books, 1988), 6.

"Inseparable": Gary Burrill, *Away: Maritimers in Massachusetts, Ontario,
and Alberta: An Oral History of Leaving Home* (Montreal &
Kingston: McGill-Queen's University Press, 1992), 4.

"*Can Anything Good Come From Halifax?*": Jayson Greene, "Rising: Ryan
Hemsworth," *Pitchfork*, January 8, 2013, accessed February 10, 2015,
pitchfork.com/features/rising/9035-ryan-hemsworth.

"Canada's most eastern provinces have the smallest populations in the
country": "Population by Year, Province, and Territory (Number),"
Statistics Canada, last modified September 29, 2015, accessed
December 22, 2015, statcan.gc.ca/tables-tableaux/sum-som/l01/
cst01/demo02a-eng.htm.

"New Brunswick, Nova Scotia, and Prince Edward Island have the lowest gross domestic product per capita": "Financial Security — Standard of Living / Indicators of Well-being in Canada," Employment and Social Development Canada, last modified January 3, 2016, accessed January 3, 2016, www4.hrsdc.gc.ca/.3ndic.1t.4r@-eng .jsp?iid=26.

"Atlantic Canadians want to support artists from home": John Demont, "Longing for Home: In Search of Nova Scotia's Soul," *Chronicle Herald Magazine*, January 25, 2014, accessed February 15, 2014, thechronicleherald.ca/heraldmagazine/1180910-longing-for-home-in-search-of-nova-scotia-s-soul.

"Like a motorcycle gang": Bruce, 46.

"In the 1750s, nearly 11,000 of them were deported": Margaret R. Conrad and James K. Hiller, *Atlantic Canada: A History* (Toronto: Oxford University Press, 2010), 79.

"The population reached 800,000 by 1861": Ibid., 107.

"The Aboriginal population in the Maritimes had by then shrunk to 3,000": Ibid., 109.

"The characteristics of a mass migration": Alan A. Brookes, "Out-Migration from the Maritime Provinces, 1860–1900: Some Preliminary Considerations," *Acadiensis* 5, no. 2 (spring 1976): 31.

"Decapitation": Judith Fingard, "The 1880s: Paradoxes of Progress," *The Atlantic Provinces in Confederation*, ed. E.R. Forbes and D.A. Muise (Toronto: University of Toronto Press, 1993), 97

"From 1851 to 1931, more than 600,000 people left the Maritimes; while there was some immigration, it was a net loss of 460,000 people": Studies cited in Patricia A. Thornton, "The Problem of Out-Migration from Atlantic Canada, 1871–1921: A New Look," *Acadiensis* 15, no. 1 (autumn 1985): 5.

"Burned two-fifths of the New Brunswick city to the ground": Donald Collins, "Weary City Resurfaces from Ashes," *New Brunswick Telegraph-Journal*, June 20, 2002.

"Roughly 2,000 people died and the city's north end was leveled": "Explosion FAQ," Maritime Museum of the Atlantic, accessed February 10, 2015, maritimemuseum.novascotia.ca/what-see-do/halifax-explosion/explosion-faq.

"'Tis clear, they can't stay here / For work to do there's none": John Cousins, "James H. Fitzgerald and 'Prince Edward Isle, Adieu,'" *The Island Magazine*, Fall/Winter 1980, 27–31.

"Farewell to Nova Scotia, the sea-bound coast": "Farewell to Nova
    Scotia / The Nova Scotia Song," Helen Creighton Folklore Society,
    accessed February 10, 2015, helencreighton.org/collection/NSsong.

"Continuing to go down the road to Central Canada to secure a job":
    Donald J. Savoie, *Visiting Grandchildren: Economic Development in
    the Maritimes* (Toronto: University of Toronto Press, 2006), 35.

"Not much changed on the east coast": "Full Text of the Atlantic
    Provinces Section of the Royal Commission on Canada's
    Economic Prospects — Preliminary Report," *Atlantic Advocate*,
    March 1957, 94.

"Maritimization": Michael Clow, "'Maritimizing' Canada: Speeding
    Up the De-Industrialization of Our Economy," *The Facts on Free
    Trade: Canada, Don't Trade It Away*, 10, no. 2 (spring 1988): 98

"New notion of happiness": David Alexander, "New Notions of Happi-
    ness: Nationalism, Regionalism, and Atlantic Canada," *Journal of
    Canadian Studies*, 15, no. 2 (1980): 40.

"The region grew less than one-tenth of a percent between 2011 and
    2015": Calculations done from Statistics Canada tables: "Population
    by Year, by Province and Territory," Statistics Canada, modified
    September 29, 2015, accessed December 22, 2015, statcan.gc.ca/
    tables-tableaux/sum-som/l01/cst01/demo02a-eng.htm.

"Meanwhile, 10 percent of the local labour force is unemployed":
    Calculations done from Statistics Canada tables: "Labour Force,
    Employment and Unemployment, Levels and Rates, by Province
    (Newfoundland and Labrador, Prince Edward Island, Nova Scotia,
    New Brunswick)," Statistics Canada, modified January 28, 2015, ac-
    cessed December 22, 2015, statcan.gc.ca/tables-tableaux/sum-som/
    l01/cst01/labor07a-eng.htm.

"Driving up and down Main Street looking for something you know
    damn well ain't there": *Goin' Down the Road,* film, directed by
    Donald Shebib (1970: Seville Pictures, re-released in 2002), DVD.

"One of Joel Plaskett's favourites": "What Canadian Comedy Means to
    Joel Plaskett," *Telefilm Canada*, March 4, 2014, accessed July 4, 2014,
    youtube.com/watch?v=XonTtQfJfJE.

"For those like fiddling folk icon Don Messer": "Don Messer," Nova
    Scotia Archives, published May 9, 2010, accessed May 31, 2015,
    novascotia.ca/archives/virtual/messer.

"Saint John's Ken Tobias": "Biography," *Ken Tobias: The Official Website*,
    accessed May 21, 2015, kentobias.ca/bio.php; Dave Bidini, *On a
    Cold Road* (Toronto: McClelland & Stewart, 1998), 218.

"Early country star Wilf Carter": Jason Schneider, *Whispering Pines: The Northern Roots of American Music . . . From Hank Snow to The Band* (Toronto: ECW Press, 2009), 15–44.

"Hank Snow, 10 years Carter's junior . . .": Ibid., 22, 34, 42.

"I figgered it would just be so wonderful": Jo Durden-Smith, "Nashville Gothic," *Maclean's*, May 1972, 61–63.

"The train is not unlike the country it runs through": Bill Howell, "What Upper Canada Has Done to Anne Murray" / "Upper Canada Romantic," *Maclean's*, May 1972, 29–30.

"The relative Maritime obscurity from whence I'd come": Anne Murray with Michael Posner, *All of Me* (Toronto: Vintage Canada, 2009), 88.

"Stompin' Tom from Skinners Pond": Tom Connors, *Stompin' Tom and the Connors Tone* (Toronto: Viking, 2000), 82.

"That song even became a recurring punchline": "Yonge Street! Part 1," posted July 18, 2010, accessed December 22, 2015, youtube.com/watch?v=FPFAAGCoJxo, and Geoff Pevere, *Canadian Cinema: Donald Shebib's Goin' Down the Road* (Toronto: University of Toronto Press, 2012), 111.

"And this skit, in turn, helped inspire a YouTube series": From a *Globe and Mail* interview with *Just Passing Through* co-creators Jeremy Larter and Geoff Read that was unpublished as of this book's press time.

"Came to him while he was far away": Liisa Ladouceur, "Canadian Classics," February 21, 2014, accessed December 22, 2015, socanmagazine.ca/features/canadian-classics.

"Alongside Cape Bretoner John Allan Cameron": Chris Gudgeon, *Stan Rogers: Northwest Passage* (Kingston: Fox Music Books, 2004), 56; Elaine Keillor, *Music in Canada: Capturing Landscape and Diversity* (Montreal and Kingston, Ontario: McGill-Queen's University Press, 2008), 272.

"The region's first punk scenes sprouted up": This paragraph's stories of early punk largely come from Sam Sutherland, *Perfect Youth: The Birth of Canadian Punk* (Toronto: ECW Press, 2012), 214–231. *Perfect Youth* offers the most definitive narrative account of early east-coast punk, but other sources have emerged to fill in more detail, including the blogs *Atlantic Punk* (atlanticpunk.blogspot .ca, accessed September 9, 2015) and *DIY Halifax* (diyhalifax .ca/2014/01/oh-hi-im-ian-and-this-is-my-first-post.html, accessed September 9, 2015). On episode 12 of Damian Abraham's *Turned*

Out a Punk podcast, Chris Murphy of Sloan suggests there are
many gaps in *Perfect Youth*'s east coast chapter, including Fredericton's Neighbourhood Watch and Halifax's System Overload, but
Murphy and Abraham acknowledge that such is the trouble with
collecting oral histories (audioboom.com/boos/2836833-episode-12-
chris-murphy-sloan, accessed September 9, 2015).

"They released a seven-inch EP": "Null Set / *New Job* (EP)," *The Museum
of Canadian Music*, accessed July 16, 2014, mocm.ca/Music/Title.
aspx?TitleId=294182.

"Maybe eight people": "08/09/84 — Halifax, NS @ NSCAD Cafeteria,"
Sonic Youth Official Website (archived interview between Thurston
Moore and Jay Ferguson from *Chart* magazine), accessed February
10, 2015, sonicyouth.com/mustang/cc/080984.html.

"Alternative music could be made in their own backyard": Michael
Barclay, Ian A.D. Jack, and Jason Schneider, *Have Not Been the
Same: The CanRock Renaissance 1985–1995*, Rev. ed. (Toronto: ECW
Press, 2011), 460.

"The band released their second album from Toronto": "Official
Releases," *Jellyfishbabies*, last modified in 2008, accessed February
10, 2015, jellyfishbabies.com/musicpage/musicpage.php.

"Co-founded the Halifax Pop Explosion music festival": "About the
Festival," *Halifax Pop Explosion Association*, last modified in 2015,
accessed February 10, 2015, halifaxpopexplosion.com/history.

"The label's catalogue included releases from": *murderecords 7" Singles
1993–1998*, album liner notes, 2013.

3. HARBOUR BOYS

"McGettigan got a fretless bass from his mother's boyfriend": "Learn to
Party," DVD documentary included in *Thrush Hermit: The Complete
Recordings*, New Scotland Records, 2010.

"Cool as hell": Description for "The Hoods" in the liner notes of *Thrush
Hermit: The Complete Recordings*, New Scotland Records, 2010.

"As he and Benvie split a pack of smokes": Liner notes, *Thrush Hermit*.

"At Halifax's Centre for Art Tapes, the band helped paint": Liner notes,
Thrush Hermit.

"We're completely prepared for a life of poverty": "Sloan & Thrush Hermit on *Street Cents*," uploaded to YouTube May 26, 2014, accessed
February 10, 2015, youtube.com/watch?v=JXuQMbMXwL4.

"Catano, meanwhile, kept playing music": Adria Young, "We've Got
an Exclusive Stream of North of America's Reissue of 'Elements

of an Incomplete Map,'" *Noisey: Music by Vice*, November 4, 2014, accessed November 6, 2014, noisey.vice.com/en_ca/blog/weve-got-an-exclusive-stream-of-north-of-americas-reissue-of-elements-of-an-incomplete-map.

"New Seattle": Everett True, "Reviewed by Everett True," *Melody Maker*, March 27, 1993, 28.

"By the end of 1993, the Seattle comparison showed up": Paul Tough, "The Next Next Seattle," *New York Times Magazine*, December 19, 1993, accessed February 10, 2015, nytimes.com/1993/12/19/magazine/the-next-next-seattle.html; Joseph Gallivan, "Nova Scotia Is the New Seattle, Definitely," *Independent*, April 1, 1993, accessed July 23, 2014, independent.co.uk/arts-entertainment/abroad-nova-scotia-is-the-new-seattle-definitely-looking-to-catch-tomorrows-sounds-today-tune-in-to-the-nova-scotia-scene-theres-nothing-fishy-about-it-says-joseph-gallivan-1452617.html.

"Anything that's the something of the something": "*The Simpsons*: *MoneyBart* Quotes" (2010), *IMDb*, accessed February 10, 2015, imdb.com/title/tt1628662/quotes.

"Halifax 'sound'": Brad Gooch, "Sleepless in Halifax," *Harper's Bazaar*, September 1993, 224–232.

4. WAITING TO BE DISCOVERED

"What kills me about you is your inability to function on the same plane of existence as the rest of us": *Mallrats*, directed by Kevin Smith (1995: View Askew Productions/Alphaville/Gramercy Pictures), DVD.

"More than 500,000 copies": "RIAA — Gold & Platinum Searchable Database," The Recording Industry Association of America, search terms: "Dumb and Dumber," accessed December 24, 2015, riaa.com/goldandplatinumdata.php?table=SEARCH.

"Deeply ashamed": Rich Terfry, *Wicked and Weird: The Amazing Tales of Buck 65* (Toronto: Doubleday Canada, 2015), 128. This book has been revealed to be a mix of both memoir and fiction, and Terfry did not respond to an interview request when this project began; the details published here were verified by others present.

"Sounds pretty good. Maybe try singing this time": Liner notes, *Thrush Hermit*.

"Do the Billy Ocean bit": "Learn to Party," *Thrush Hermit*.

"Smudging pop-rock songs": Jon Pareles, "Pop Review; A Visit to the '70s Without a Goodbye," *New York Times*, November 4, 1995, accessed July 23, 2014, nytimes.com/1995/11/04/arts/pop-review-a-visit-to-the-70-s-without-a-goodbye.html.

"The media had begun referring to the city's Seattle-like hype in the past tense": Mark Lepage, "Toast Sampler Recalls Era When Halifax Was 'Seattle East,' *Montreal Gazette*, January 7, 1995, D7.

"Close to 7,000 people": From interview with Jeff Cohen, who was there as an agent representing 13 Engines.

"Stroke of genius": Neil Davidson, "Thrush Hermit Steals the Show at Edgefest," *Montreal Gazette*, August 7, 1995, B6.

"Kaye died in 2006": "A Sad Day," *Punk Turns 30*, October 27, 2006, accessed July 10, 2014, punkturns30.blogspot.ca/2006_10_01_archive.html.

"Had even begun to wrap the headstock of his bass with tissue paper": "Getting Real: A Talk with Joel Plaskett," *Panic Manual*, December 14, 2012, accessed September 19, 2015, panicmanual.com/2012/12/14/getting-real-a-talk-with-joel-plaskett.

"I think we found our own sound": Greg Hubert, "These Songbirds Are No Misers," *University of Western Ontario Gazette*, October 9, 1997, accessed August 22, 2014, usc.uwo.ca/gazette/1997/October/9/Entertainment2.htm.

"But for the rest of 1996, they mostly laid low": Christopher Waters, "Two Tales of a City," *Exclaim!*, February 1997, 28.

5. SNUBBED

"Sense of honest fun and big guitar-riffing bubbles": Jennie Punter, "Thrush Hermit: *Sweet Homewrecker*," *Toronto Star*, February 8, 1997, M6.

"Behind the scenes, too, changes were happening": John Seabrook, *The Song Machine: Inside the Hit Factory* (New York: W.W. Norton & Company, 2015), 77–80.

"Just a year after Elektra cut ties with Thrush Hermit": John Cook with Mac McCaughan and Laura Ballance, *Our Noise: The Story of Merge Records, the Indie Label That Got Big and Stayed Small* (Chapel Hill: Algonquin Books, 2009), 63, 172–173.

"Nice little scoot": Ian McGettigan in *Bikini* magazine, excerpted in the liner notes of *Thrush Hermit: The Complete Recordings*, New Scotland Records, 2010.

"He began drumming with them in 1998": "Neuseiland," *CBC Music*, accessed February 10, 2015, music.cbc.ca/#/artists/NEUSEILAND.

"Balls-out rock 'n' roll extravaganza": Adam M. Anklewicz, "Noosed and Haloed Swear Words," *Never Had to Fight*, March 24, 2010, accessed February 10, 2015, neverhadtofight.com/2010/03/noosed-and-haloed-swear-words.

"The *Toronto Star* loved it": Ben Rayner, "Canada's Music Awards Give Us Plenty of Fodder for Sounding Off at the Water Cooler," *Toronto Star*, March 21, 2000, ENO1.

"Important people": "Old News," *Alt.rock: A Toronto show guide*, July 13, 1998, accessed February 10, 2015, altrawk.tripod.com/scanning/oldnews.htm.

"Decidedly au naturale": "The Story of the Band Called Thrush Hermit," MapleMusic, accessed February 10, 2015, maplemusic.com/artists/thr/bio.asp.

"He'd carry rigs of lighting": "Final Show" and "From the Back of the Film," *Damage for Damage Done*, DVD, *Thrush Hermit: The Complete Recordings*.

"The Hermit announced their split on September 21, 1999": "Thrush Hermit," *CBC Music*, accessed February 10, 2015, music.cbc.ca/artists/Thrush-Hermit.

"I'm quite fond of it": "Historian Sharon MacDonald Gives a Slide Lecture," *Toronto Star*, April 24, 2000, LIO1.

"A star": James Oldham, "Future Stars and Stripes," *New Musical Express*, October 2, 1999, 33.

"Thinkers. We sometimes overthought things": Natalie Flute, "A Bid Farewell to the Legendary Hermit," *Pro Tem: Glendon's Bilingual Newspaper*, January 31, 2000, 10, accessed as PDF February 10, 2015, pi.library.yorku.ca/ojs/index.php/protem/article/viewFile/16096/15001.

"In practice, a huge pain": Jon Fine, *Your Band Sucks: What I Saw at Indie Rock's Failed Revolution (But Can No Longer Hear)* (New York: Viking Penguin, 2015), 182.

"And even though he'd long been sequestered to stage right": Mike Campbell, "Final Show," *Damage for Damage Done*, DVD, *Thrush Hermit: The Complete Recordings*, 2010.

6. WORK OUT FINE

"This included making a debut full-length for Neuseiland": Ian Danzig, "Neuseiland: *Neuseiland*," *Exclaim!*, June 1, 2000, accessed January 10, 2015, exclaim.ca/Reviews/ImprovAndAvantGarde/neuseiland-neuseiland.

"Music historian Bob Mersereau listed *Down at the Khyber* as No. 46": Tom Harrison, "Why 100 Albums? Why Now?; Bob Mersereau's Book Is a Rite of Passage for Canadian Pop," *National Post*, October, 22, 2007, AL6.

"Stands out among the punk-bred musicians": Carl Wilson, "Obsessed with the Craft of Rock," *Globe and Mail*, August 2, 2001, R4.

"Need-to-know guitar-rock triumph": Quoted in Carl Wilson, "An Honest Day's Song. Halifax Singer-Songwriter Joel Plaskett Wants to Be Truthful to Listeners," *Globe and Mail*, November 1, 2003, R19.

"The manager who put a rock band behind fiddler Ashley MacIsaac in 1994": Rebecca Mead, "Sex, Drugs, and Fiddling," *The New Yorker*, December 1999, accessed on September 19, 2015, web.archive.org/web/20050207133405/http://rebeccamead.com/1999_12_20_art_ashley.htm (previewable at newyorker.com/magazine/1999/12/20/sex-drugs-and-fiddling).

"Woe-is-me": Wilson, "An Honest Day's Song."

"I take a certain amount of pride living out here": Michael Barclay, "The Restlessly Rooted Life of Joel Plaskett," *Exclaim!*, January 1, 2006, accessed February 10, 2015, exclaim.ca/Interviews/From TheMagazine/restlessly_rooted_life_of_joel_plaskett.

"If F. Scott Fitzgerald famously claimed that there are no second acts in American lives": Wilson, "An Honest Day's Song."

"They have the sentimental side down pat": Jordan Zivitz, "New Music: Newly Released Compact Discs: Joel Plaskett Emergency: *Truthfully Truthfully*," *Montreal Gazette*, November 27, 2003, D2.

"They packed Lee's Palace in Toronto": Alan Niester, "Truthfully, a Star Emerges," *Globe and Mail*, November 22, 2003, R14.

7. HAPPEN NOW

"People celebrate it": Brad Wheeler, "Songs That Take Us Home," *Globe and Mail*, March 21, 2012, R4.

"*La De Da* might have warranted a trip away": Vish Khanna, "Joel Plaskett: *La De Da*," *Exclaim!*, March 1, 2005, accessed August 31 2015, exclaim.ca/Music/article/joel_plaskett-la_de_da.

"Jaw-dropping": Trevor Savory, "Joel Plaskett: '*La De Da*,'" *The Coast*, December 6, 2007, accessed February 10, 2015, thecoast.ca/halifax/joel-plaskett/Content?oid=964818.

"Among his best works": Khanna, "Plaskett," 2005.

"Doesn't undercut its pop appeal": J.D. Considine, "Escapist Pleasures of Snowbird Rock," *Globe and Mail*, March 4, 2005, R30.

"The growing number of parallels to Bruce Springsteen": Joshua Errett,
   "Tall Poppy Interview — Joel Plaskett, Musician," *Torontoist*, April
   26, 2005, accessed February 10, 2015, torontoist.com/2005/04/
   tall_poppy_inte_6.
"The lanky songwriter had taken the Charlottetown band Two Hours
   Traffic under his wing": "Producer Credits," Joel Plaskett, accessed
   February 10, 2015, joelplaskett.com/producer-credits.
"In bars and online, hipsters started invigorated debates": "Duff = Plas-
   kett," Giraffecycle.com (New Brunswick Music Discussion Board),
   June 2006, accessed February 10, 2015, giraffecycle.com/forum/
   viewtopic.php?t=14662&highlight=&sid=026a28d407b65ca6be
   c0aa69734855e9.
"The song remains the Emergency's best seller on iTunes": "Make a
   Little Noise EP," iTunes Store, accessed September 1, 2015, itunes
   .apple.com/ca/album/nowhere-with-you/id129536370?i=129536379.

8. SOUNDTRACK FOR THE NIGHT
The origins of the *Ashtray Rock* songs can be found in the liner notes
   of *Thrush Hermit: The Complete Recordings* (New Scotland Records,
   2010); the liner notes for *Emergencys, false alarms, shipwrecks, castaways, fragile creatures, special features, demons and demonstrations:
   1999–2010* (New Scotland Records, 2011); and in Michael Barclay,
   "Joel Plaskett," *Radio Free Canuckistan*, May 24, 2007, accessed
   September 15, 2015, radiofreecanuckistan.blogspot.ca/2007/05/
   joel-plaskett.html.
"Elvis Costello transplanted into a Canadian garage band": Guy Dixon,
   "Dark Horses Make Polaris Short List," *Globe and Mail*, July 11,
   2007.
"'Fashionable People' went on to win the Billboard World Songwriting
   Contest": Brock Thiessen, "Joel Plaskett Wins Billboard World
   Songwriting Contest," *Exclaim!*, February 20, 2008, accessed July
   29, 2014, exclaim.ca/News/joel_plaskett_wins_billboard_world_
   songwriting.
"Heartfelt and exuberant": Allison Outhit, "Joel Plaskett — *Ashtray
   Rock*," *Exclaim!*, July 23, 2007, accessed February 10, 2015, exclaim
   .ca/Features/Research/joel_plaskett-_ashtray_rock.
"Closer than he's ever been to the icon": Adam Radwanski, "Legend of
   Ashtray Rock Burns On," *National Post*, May 25, 2007, accessed
   February 10, 2015, canada.com/cityguides/toronto/story.html?id=7c
   cc1c35-a2e0-458e-ba3c-093f083e2cf5&k=2429.

"Absorbing, charming, entertaining, and moving": Ross Langager, "Joel
    Plaskett Emergency: *Ashtray Rock*," *PopMatters*, April 2, 2008,
    accessed February 10, 2015, popmatters.com/review/joel-
    plaskett-emergency-ashtray-rock.
"Funny, smart, and heartbreaking": Mark Deming, "*Ashtray Rock*,"
    AllMusic, accessed February 10, 2015, allmusic.com/album/ashtray-
    rock-mw0001904243.
"This album just feels like home": Ryan McNutt, "Hitting Home With
    Plaskett's *Ashtray Rock*," *McNutt Against the Music*, April 19, 2007,
    accessed February 10, 2015, mcnutt.wordpress.com/2007/04/19/in-
    which-mcnutt-reviews-ashtray-rock.

9. EVERY TIME YOU LEAVE

"He listened in amazement at their combined voices": Sean Flinn, "Joel
    Plaskett: Three for the road," *The Coast*, May 28, 2009, accessed
    February 10, 2015, thecoast.ca/halifax/joel-plaskett-three-for-the-
    road/Content?oid=1130704.
"A recording engineer who'd worked with": "Recording Credits," *Ken
    Friesen*, accessed September 1, 2015, kenfriesen.com/credits.
"Quahogs singer Scott Tappen": Stephanie Johns, "Our Poster Past," *The
    Coast*, October 24, 2013, accessed February 10, 2015, thecoast.ca/
    halifax/our-poster-past/Content?oid=4106848.
"Plaskett wrote a hook inspired by his obsessiveness over the ses-
    sions": Mark Medley, "Joel Plaskett: Two Can Be as Bad as One,"
    National Post, March 26, 2009, accessed February 10, 2015,
    nationalpost.com/arts/story.html?id=1419461.
"Going Gold within six months": "Gold/Platinum search for Joel
    Plaskett," *Music Canada*, accessed February 9, 2015, musiccanada
    .com/gold-platinum/?fwp_gp_search=joel%20plaskett.
"Simply a great reminder of Joel Plaskett's singular talent": Vish Khanna,
    "Joel Plaskett: *Three*," *Exclaim!*, March 26, 2009, accessed February
    10, 2015, exclaim.ca/Reviews/PopAndRock/joel_plaskett-three.
"Ambitious, but it doesn't overreach": Frank Yang, "Rollin' Rollin'
    Rollin'," *Chromewaves*, May 13, 2009, accessed February 10, 2015,
    chromewaves.net/2009/05/review-of-joel-plasketts-three-and-
    giveaway.
"A spell of personal storytelling, easy-breezy harmonies, and Wester-
    bergian rock": Sue Carter Flinn, "Best Vinyl [2010]: Joel Plaskett,
    Three," *The Coast*, accessed February 10, 2015, thecoast.ca/halifax/
    best-vinyl-of-2009/BestOf?oid=1577529.

"A new CanCon classic": Brendan Murphy, "Joel Plaskett: *Three* — Disc Review," *The Hour,* April 23, 2009, accessed February 10, 2015, hour. ca/2009/04/23/three-2.

"Plaskett is incredibly gifted, incredibly prolific": Wilfrid Langmaid, "Plaskett's *Three* Is 'Personal, Transfixing,'" *Daily Gleaner*, April 25, 2009, D5.

"Twenty-six thousand people showed up to the Halifax Common": Tim Bosquet, "Two Decades of World-Class Delusion," *The Coast*, July 11 2013, accessed September 1, 2015, thecoast.ca/halifax/two-decades-of-world-class-delusion/Content?oid=3930595.

10. TIME FLIES

"Plaskett confirmed to media": Vish Khanna, "Exclusive: Joel Plaskett Confirms Thrush Hermit Reunion," *Exclaim!*, December 14, 2009, accessed February 10, 2015, exclaim.ca/News/exclusive_joel_plaskett_confirms_thrush_hermit_reunion.

"The band announced a box set, *The Complete Recordings*, in February": Keith Carman, "Thrush Hermit Announced Retrospective Seven-Disc Box Set," *Exclaim!*, February 8, 2010, accessed February 10, 2015, exclaim.ca/News/thrush_hermit_announce_retrospective_seven-disc_box_set_2.

"The classic lineup": Cam Lindsay, "Thrush Hermit, Lee's Palace, Toronto, ON, March 26," *Exclaim!*, March 27, 2010, accessed February 10, 2015, exclaim.ca/Reviews/Concerts/Thrush_Hermit-Lees_Palace_Toronto_on_March_26; Carla Gillis, "Thrush Hermit Flies Again," *NOW Magazine*, March 24, 2010, accessed February 10, 2015, nowtoronto.com/music/story.cfm?content=174262.

"It's more important murderecords or Cinnamon Toast Records exists": "HPX94," MuchMusic 1994 Halifax Pop Explosion Special, uploaded to YouTube October 14 2010, accessed February 10, 2015, youtube.com/watch?v=qvvnGP_Qdho.

"At the studio, Plaskett also wrote and recorded 'On the Rail'": "Great Canadian Song Quest Final Songs Debut on CBC Radio 2 Drive," *CBC Radio 2*, November 24, 2009, accessed February 10, 2015, cbc.ca/bc/community/blog/media-releases/Song%20Quest%20Titles%20Release%20-%20BC.pdf.

"This time, Plaskett found inspiration with 'On the Rail'": Kenzie Love, "This Is an Emergency," *FFWD Weekly*, April 12, 2013, accessed February 10, 2015, ffwdweekly.com/article/music/music-previews/this-is-an-emergency-8980.

"Rough-around-the-edges": Ben Rayner, "Joel Plaskett and his singles file," *Toronto Star*, May 17, 2012, accessed December 22, 2015, thestar. com/entertainment/music/2012/05/17/joel_plaskett_and_his_singles_file.html.

"Unbridled joy": Stephen Cooke, "Plaskett lands in New Glasgow," *Halifax Chronicle-Herald*, August, 1 2012, accessed December 22, 2015, thechronicleherald.ca/artslife/122708-plaskett-lands-in-new-glasgow.

"Halifax's Rick Rubin": Adria Young, "Joel Plaskett, Halifax's Rick Rubin, Showed Us His Analog Studio," *Noisey: Music by Vice*, November 3, 2014, accessed November 3, 2014, noisey.vice.com/en_ca/blog/joel-plaskett-halifaxs-rick-rubin-showed-us-his-analog-studio.

"Voted to keep it under the city's stewardship": Brett Bundale, "Khyber Saved: Halifax Council Seeks Ways to Maintain Arts and Culture Hub," *The Chronicle Herald*, September 9 2014, accessed September 9, 2014, thechronicleherald.ca/metro/1235172-khyber-saved-halifax-council-seeks-ways-to-maintain-arts-and-culture-hub.

Much of the detail regarding the recording of The Park Avenue Sobriety Test, as well as several quotes by Joel Plaskett, Kim Cooke, and Peter Elkas, comes from interviews conducted for a *Globe and Mail* feature, and I am grateful to the paper for letting me reuse this information. Josh O'Kane, "Joel Plaskett's New Album Is a Veritable Kitchen Party," *Globe and Mail*, March 13, 2015, accessed April 28, 2015, theglobeandmail.com/arts/music/joel-plasketts-new-album-is-a-veritable-kitchen-party/article23445724.

"He became the first artist to reach a million on-demand plays": Facebook post by CBC Radio 3, May 31, 2011, accessed February 10, 2015, facebook.com/cbcradio3/posts/220281831333576.

"True pioneer of the Canadian music scene": Emma Godmere, "Plaskett Primer: The Top 15 Songs by 2014 Lifetime Achievement Award Winner Joel Plaskett," *CBC Music*, December 5, 2013, accessed December 5, 2013, music.cbc.ca/#/blogs/2013/12/Plaskett-primer-the-top-15-songs-by-2013-Lifetime-Achievement-Bucky-Award-winner-Joel-Plaskett. (Full disclosure: I was consulted for the construction of this playlist.)

"Contrast that with the award he received": Lezlie Lowe, "Best of Halifax 2002: Most Likely to Move to Toronto: Joel Plaskett," *The Coast*, accessed February 10, 2015, thecoast.ca/halifax/most-likely-to-move-to-toronto/BestOf?oid=3867476 and thecoast.ca/halifax/most-likely-to-move-to-toronto/BestOf?oid=3867525.

PERMISSIONS